DISCARDED

"*My Life with Che* offers an intimate look at one of the most influential figures of the Cuban Revolution. The story of Che's life has become inseparable from the myth, and this book sheds new light on the man from the unique perspective of his first wife Hilda Gadea."

—Alfredo José Estrada, author of
Havana: Autobiography of a City

"Gadea's insights into the thinking and behavior of the young Che, and the Castro brothers during their exile in Mexico in the mid-1950s, are of great historical value. Che was then perfecting his Marxist beliefs but Raul Castro was already a great admirer of the Soviet Union. Gadea reveals too that Fidel espoused a radical internationalist agenda that he concealed from the Cuban people until after his victory. Essential reading for anyone interested in the Cuban revolution."

—Brian Latell, author of
After Fidel: Raul Castro and the Future of Cuba's Revolution and
Senior Research Associate in Cuban Studies at the University of Miami

"A candid, serious memoir by the iconic revolutionary's first wife [who] . . . met Ernesto Guevara in Guatemala on December 20, 1953. . . . A kinship developed between the like-minded two, as they shared Marxist tomes and ideas on how to resist the imperialist oligarchies controlling most of Latin America. . . . Gadea and Guevara married and had a daughter, Hildita, but the revolution ultimately separated them. . . . An intelligent, tender look at Guevara's human side."

—*Kirkus Reviews*

MY LIFE WITH CHE

MY LIFE WITH CHE

The Making of a Revolutionary

HILDA GADEA

palgrave
macmillan

First published in English in 1972 by Doubleday & Company

This edition published in 2008 by
PALGRAVE MACMILLAN®—a division of St. Martin's Press
LLC, 175 Fifth Avenue, New York, N.Y. 10010.

Palgrave Macmillan is the global academic imprint of the above
companies and has companies and representatives throughout
the world.

Palgrave® and Macmillan® are registered trademarks in the
United States, the United Kingdom, Europe and other countries.

ISBN-13: 978-0-230-60601-2
ISBN-10: 0-230-60601-6

Gadea, Hilda.
    [Che Guevara. English]
    My life with Che : the making of a revolutionary / Hilda
Gadea.
        p.   cm.
    Includes index.
    ISBN 0-230-60601-6
    1. Guevara, Ernesto, 1928–1967.   2. Guevara, Ernesto,
1928–1967—Family.   3. Gadea, Hilda.   4. Revolutionaries—
Latin America—Biography.   5. Revolutionaries' spouses—
Latin America—Biography.   I. Title.
    F2849.22.G85G2713   2008
    980.03'5092—dc22

                                              2008003325

A catalogue record of the book is available from the British
Library.

Design by Letra Libre, Inc.

First Palgrave Macmillan edition: August 2008
10 9 8 7 6 5 4 3 2 1
Printed in the United States of America.

CONTENTS

We only ask of the narrator that he be strictly truthful, that he never say anything inexact in order to enhance his personal position or to imply his presence at a certain place. We ask that, each one, on writing his notes in the best form of which he is capable according to his education and disposition, then very carefully edit these and eliminate any words which do not refer to a strictly true fact, or of whose veracity the author is not fully confident. It is with that spirit that we begin our recollections.

—*Ernesto "Che" Guevara, Prologue to*
Passages of the Revolutionary War

ACKNOWLEDGMENTS

To Mr. Ralph Schoenman, Director of Studies in the Third World, who encouraged me to write this book; to Myrna Torres, who verified dates and places; and to Juan Aguilar Derpich, for copying my drafts and making helpful comments.

TIMELINE OF EVENTS

March 1921	Hilda Gadea Acosta is born in Lima, Peru
1946	Gadea graduates with an economics degree
1948	Manuel A. Odria takes power and Hilda is forced into exile in Guatemala
December 1953	Gadea meets Ernesto Guevara
January 1954	Gadea introduces Guevara to the Cubans of the 26th of July Movement
March 1954	Guevara proposes for the first time
October 1954	Guatemalan president Jacobo Arbenz is overthrown by coup d'etat; Gadea joins Guevara in Mexico
January 1955	Gadea accepts Guevara's marriage proposal
September 1955	Hilda Gadea marries Ernesto Guevara
February 1956	Gadea gives birth to Hilda Beatríz "Hildita" Guevara in Mexico City

November 1956   Fidel Castro, Che Guevara, and the rest of the Cuban revolutionaries leave to invade Cuba on the *Granma,* arriving December 2

January 1959   Gadea and Hildita join Guevara in Cuba

May 1959   Gadea and Guevara divorce

October 1967   Ernesto "Che" Guevara is executed in Bolivia

February 1974   Hilda Gadea dies in Havana, Cuba

August 1995   Hildita Guevara dies in Havana, Cuba

FOREWORD

HILDA BENITA GADEA ACOSTA, *la China,* as we called her, was born in an old house in downtown Lima on March 21, 1921, the eldest of six siblings. All her life she was known as an idealist, a woman with a strong temperament—dynamic, enthusiastic, extremely intelligent and with ideas that were far ahead of her time.

Hilda studied in Lima, finished high school in 1938, and immediately enrolled in a one-year program to become a technical accountant. At the same time, with great dedication, she studied French, English, and German. Some years later, these studies would allow her to read the classics in their original languages with Ernesto.

In 1940, Hilda was admitted to the Major National Univerisity of San Marcos, South America's oldest university. She studied Economics, earning degrees as a Public Accountant in 1944 and as an Economist in 1946. People who met her during those years remember her as a brilliant student, despite her financial hardships.

Our family could not afford to pay for Hilda's studies so she always had to support herself—she worked as a secretary, an assistant accountant, and as a translator. In 1946, the same year she graduated from college, Hilda also started a small family business called *Amarilis,* a hairdressing salon for ladies, in downtown Lima.

WHAT DEFINED HILDA'S LIFE was her early involvement in politics. At a time when very few Peruvian women dared to demand their rights as citizens and to break conventions based on chauvinism, she took a bold political and social stance. Some of Hilda's contemporaries vividly remember her activism and leadership during the student marches against the dictatorship of General Oscar Benavides, who governed Peru from 1933 to 1939.

While in college, Hilda quickly became known for her work with the American Popular Revolutionary Alliance's (Alianza Popular Revolucionaria Americana, or APRA) University Youth movement, known as the JAU. Hilda was a combative and powerful speaker and soon became a student leader and a member of the political cadre of the Juventud Aprista Peruana (JAP), to which JAU belonged. On several occasions she was elected student representative.

After the final defeat of Benavides' government, the APRA began to lead popular revolts against the oligarchic government of Manuel Prado, which lasted from 1939 to 1945. The student movement was one of the fundamental pillars in this effort. This popular opposition to Prado's government played a decisive role in the electoral victory of the Democratic Front headed by José Luis Bustamante y Rivero.

The new government opened a short democratic parenthesis (1945–1948) that made the APRA party and the Communist party legal. APRA founder Víctor Raúl Haya de la Torre returned from exile, and the APRA won their first parliamentary majority.

Because of her outstanding work in the youth and student organizations, during the Second National Congress of the APRA on May 1, 1948, Hilda was awarded an extraordinary honor. She was elected national secretary of statistics at age twenty-seven, thus becoming the youngest member and one of the only two women to belong to the National Executive Committee of APRA, one of the most important Latin American parties at the time.

Nevertheless, the democratic promise of the Bustamante y Rivero government soon shipwrecked. The oligarchs conspired with army leaders to overthrow the government and Bustamante seemed hesitant to quell the conspiracy. With limited resources, the APRA bases and the military constitutionalists prepared to fight the military coup.

On October 3, 1948, there was an insurrection at the Navy Base of Callao. The Marines rose in a confused, disorganized effort that was brutally quashed by the army. The oligarchs accused the APRA leaders, who had not in fact endorsed the rebellion, of attempting to take power by force. This was the perfect excuse for the military coup led by General Manuel A. Odría, launched in Arequipa[1] on October 27.

Odría's new dictatorship unleashed a brutal persecution against people's organizations. The APRA was immediately declared illegal. As one of its first measures, the military government dictated a confinement order for all APRA leaders. Thousands of militants were taken to concentration camps, and many were tortured and assassinated. Hilda went underground to avoid this same fate.

During the terrifying first weeks of persecution, Hilda hid in the homes of party comrades and friends from San Marcos. She eventually obtained asylum at the Guatemalan embassy in Lima. The ambassador and his family cordially received Hilda, and during her short stay they developed a great affection for her. After securing a safe-conduct pass from the coup authorities, Hilda left for Guatemala on Christmas Day, 1948.

IN OCTOBER 1944 Guatemala was living through a period of hopeful democratic process, which followed the dictatorships of generals

---

1.   General Manuel A. Odría's revolution lasted from 1948 to 1956.

Ubico[2] and Ponce.[3] A year later, in the first free elections of its history, a teacher, Juan José Arévalo, was elected president of the republic, promoting a program of economic and social reforms. The so-called October Revolution gave rise to enormous expectations for change and justice for the people of Guatemala.

In Guatemala, Hilda began working as an economist at the Institute of Promotion for Production (INFOP), an organization created by the government to provide financial credit to peasants. She earned a modest salary, equivalent to around US$350 a month, which, according to her closest friends, she spent very carefully.

People exiled with Hilda in Guatemala remember that she was extremely selfless in both her professional and political work for the sibling country that had welcomed her. Many APRA leaders were exiled in Guatemala during the same period, and they created the Committee of Apristas in Exile, electing Hilda as their secretary of social assistance.

When Juan José Arévalo's mandate expired in 1950, democratic elections were held and Colonel Jacobo Árbenz assumed the presidency. The main platform of his campaign while running for election was agrarian reform, demanded by the peasant majority. Since the lands belonging to the United Fruit Company—which owned the largest estate in Guatemala, and in the whole of Central America—were affected by these reforms, Guatemala became the target of the aggressive maneuvers by the United States, which denigrated the country, calling it an advance test of "communist

---

2.   The dictator General Jorge Ubico governed his country for fourteen years, from 1930 to 1944.

3.   General Federico Ponce temporarily assumed leadership of the government for three months after Ubico was overthrown, in a vain attempt to maintain the status quo.

intervention" in the continent. Meanwhile, solidarity for this unusual democratic revolution kept growing in the international community.

Hilda managed to gather a good number of Latin American militants who had sought shelter in this democratic oasis. Peruvians, Hondurans, Nicaraguans, Venezuelans, Cubans, with the most diverse political experiences, formed a large, friendly group; men and women of different countries, animated by great social passions and revolutionary ideas. By the end of 1953, Hilda had introduced Ernesto Guevara and Eduardo "Gualo" García (who had been traveling with him through South America) to this restless group of young people.

Hilda was very skilled at convincing her friends to aid the political exiles; she organized parties, hikes, cultural and other activities. Myrna Torres, daughter of the great Nicaraguan intellectual Edelberto Torres and a very close friend of Hilda's, remembered:

> Through Hilda we met the Cuban exiles who had taken part in the assault on the Moncada Quarter: Antonio Ñico Lopez, Arming Arencibia, Galician Antonio Lopez and Mario Dalmau. Also two other Cubans, Benjamin de Yurre, an authentic,[4] who later on became secretary to President Urrutia during the Cuban Revolution, and Jose Manuel Vega, Cheché. The former were really good revolutionaries, although not very prepared; the latter were nice and we all became good friends. But, the one I came to truly appreciate as a brother was Ñico Lopez.
>
> Through Hilda I also met many exiles from Venezuela, Peru and Honduras, but the ones who made the biggest impression on me and my friends were the Argentineans Ernesto Guevara and Eduardo García, who stood out for their simplicity and natural demeanor.

---

4. Of the Authentic Movement, led by Raúl Chibás.

The relationship between Hilda and Ernesto Guevara heated up against the backdrop of the decisive political events that took place in Guatemala. A strong attraction grew between them, based on ideals and love. This relationship lasted three years, until the definitive departure of Che on the *Granma*.

Hilda, a veteran militant and exiled leader of one of the main Latin American parties of the time, and Ernesto, a man of vast intellectual and political talent, but without previous experience in a party, agreed in their revolutionary vision. The flagrant intervention of the United States in Guatemala defined their relationship as a couple and forced them to flee to Mexico.

During these decisive years in Guatemala and Mexico, Ernesto and Hilda shared many happy experiences—infinite debates on literature and politics, friends, trips, the encounter with the Cubans of the Moncada Barracks, their marriage in Tepotzotlán and the birth of Hildita, or "little Mao," as well as terrible moments—the sly attack against Guatemala and the overthrow of Árbenz, the government's repression, Hilda's imprisonment, the secrecy and jail time surrounding her escape to Mexico shortly before the invasion of Cuba. All these things were compounded by their eventual separation: Hilda could not board the *Granma* because she had to take care of their newborn daughter.

HILDA RETURNED TO Peru with her daughter, after 8 years of exile, in December 1956. I almost could not remember her and felt as if I was meeting her for the first time. I knew that my sister was wholly dedicated to politics, which seemed very audacious and dangerous at the time, but I had not imagined that she enjoyed cooking and took care of Hildita with so much love. With Hilda's help I took my first "political" steps: I was a cadet of the Leoncio Prado Military Academy and she convinced me to teach math to several groups of young *apristas*.

Odría's dictatorship had come to an end with the second rise to power of Manuel Prado.[5] Hilda realized that inside the APRA the discord regarding the use of the party's original positions was getting worse. In particular, the controversy over whether APRA could continue to coexist with *pradismo*—the price that the party had to pay for its return to legality—was severe.

During the Third National Congress of the APRA in July 1957, Hilda was reelected National Secretary of Statistics and was made a member of the National Executive Committee. With the partial approval of party leaders she promoted party-wide support of and solidarity with the Cuban Revolution. Even though this cause was not viewed favorably by the old leaders, who feared an expansion of the revolution, the guerrillas of Sierra Maestra roused the fervor of the Aprista youth.

Hilda represented the 26th of July Movement in Peru until the victory of the guerrillas in Cuba. She then started the movement for the liberation of Cuba, with the support of the leftist current within the APRA. She welcomed several exiled and persecuted Cubans to Lima. Her activity became truly intense: she organized press conferences, promoted encounters and debates, and streamlined moral and material support for the combatants.

Nevertheless, she was not satisfied with her role of supporter in the rear. On February 15, 1958, the day Hildita turned two, Hilda wrote to Ernesto, declaring her intention to join the guerrilla warfare in the mountains of Cuba. His answer took several months to arrive. Che replied that the time was not right because the war was entering a decisive phase with the offensive of Sierra Maestra

5.   On June 6, 1956, Prado received political amnesty and returned to govern Peru from 1956 to 1962.

against Las Villas and that he himself would not be in a permanent place.[6]

With the success of the revolution, Hilda traveled with her little daughter to Havana as soon as she could.[7] After waiting through the popular uprising, the coming together of the masses, and the implementation of the initial revolutionary laws, she was finally reunited with Ernesto, who, thanks to his own merits, had become one of the main leaders of the *real revolution.* Their dreams had finally come true.

In the midst of the joy of victory and their reunion, Ernesto told Hilda frankly that he was committed to another woman who he had met during the war, a terrible shock for Hilda. She suffered without consolation but also understood that destiny had separated them. She decided to continue her political life in Cuba and Peru.

Hilda and Ernesto eventually divorced in May 1959, by mutual consent. As she proudly remembered later, she did not request or demand anything from Ernesto. In spite of their separation, they maintained a friendly relationship because of Hildita and their common revolutionary ideals and objectives.

Hilda's first job in Cuba was at the Institute for Agrarian Reform (INRA), an organization that supported the construction of new houses for the peasants affected by the bombings and retaliatory attacks of Batista's army. Later she worked for several years at the Cuban government's national press agency, *Prensa Latina,* in the department of economic information, as part of an outstanding group of economists, who warmly remember her humane and professional qualities.

---

6. Led by the commandants Ernesto Che Guevara and Camilo Cienfuegos, the offensive divided the island and ended with the taking of Havana and overthrow of Fulgencio Batista.

7. Hilda arrived in Havana on January 21, 1959.

Hilda stayed informed about the evolution of the APRA party. At first the official representatives of the party—who saw with increasing concern the radicalization of the anti-imperialistic trend of the revolution—were invited to Cuba. By her own account, Hilda talked to Ernesto and obtained an invitation for the leftist leaders of the old party, the "rebellious *apristas*," who identified themselves with the path of the Cuban process.

During the Fourth National Convention of the APRA in October 1959, the tension escalated. One of the main Aprista leaders, Luis de la Puente Uceda, and his followers were expelled from the party. The "rebellious APRA" formally split from Haya de la Torre's party. By the end of December 1959, Hilda publicly resigned from the APRA, the party of her youth, with a letter from Lima:

> *I am convinced that our people are finding their own path to liberation, in spite of those who go, voluntarily or involuntarily, in the opposite direction. As the great Guatemalan teacher and continental leader, doctor Juan José Arévalo, said in his recent stay in Havana: "In this moment in time there are only two paths in Latin America: the one of Fidel Castro and Muñoz Marín—the path of dignity and national sovereignty—and the path of deceit."*

Always consistent with her ideals, Hilda broke with the new direction in which the APRA was headed and took up the cause of the Cuban and Latin American Revolutions. In the following years she dedicated all her energies to the consolidation of the Cuban process and to the encouragement of the revolutionary efforts in Peru and in other Latin American countries.

The door of Hilda's home, on Fifth Avenue at Thirty-second Street in Miramar, was always open to friends and comrades. As in Guatemala and Mexico, Hilda offered her friendship and welcomed many revolutionaries from around the continent.

When I went to Cuba in 1960, I had the good fortune to meet some remarkable characters at Hilda's home: people like Brazilian leader Francisco Julião, future Chilean president Salvador Allende, North American writer Harold White, Cuban-Spanish Commander Armando Bayo, and Peruvians Juan Gonzalo Rose and Luis de la Puente.

Frequently, at least twice or three times a week, Che would come home to visit Hildita, taking her out for a walk or sometimes staying in for a cup of coffee. Until 1961, when the Peruvian government broke diplomatic relations with Cuba, Hilda traveled to Lima many times, seeking reconciliation between the two leftist forces. Héctor Lamb Guevara, one of the historical leaders of the "rebellious APRA," remembered her eagerness:

> Since the police would follow her wherever she went, I would pick her up at a previously determined secret place; she would hide under the seat of my truck and from there enter the house where we had set up a meeting. She was an exemplary fighter, optimistic, honest in her appreciations and consistent with her ideals. . . .

In Peru, Hilda supported the rebellious *aprismo* that founded the Revolutionary Left Movement (MIR), led by Luis de la Puente,[8] one of the most important forces of the Peruvian left. At that time, Fernando Belaúnde Terry, leader of the Popular Action (AP) party, was president of the country (1963–1968). The new government represented the reformist bourgeoisie and the ideology of the Alliance for Progress, which was initiated by the United States, whose aim it was to subvert the dangerous example of the Cuban revolution. Nonetheless, the regime had to come to terms with both the right-wing oligarchic parties and the left-wing APRA, which con-

---

8.   The MIR was founded in 1962. It abandoned APRA's ideology to assume one that embraced Marxism and the fight for socialism.

trolled the parliament. Faced with mounting pressure from popular movements, the regime resorted to repression.

The MIR organized its bases in the provinces, mainly in the regions where the tradition of agrarian struggle was strongest. In 1965,[9] denouncing the treason of Belaunde's regime, it united a guerrilla movement and formed several fronts, rousing the country with their anti-imperialistic program and the promise of an agrarian revolution. The Peruvian army, one of the most proficient armies in fighting counterinsurgencies on the continent, faced extreme difficulties in its struggle against the guerrillas, despite the immense disparity of resources. A year later, with the deaths of Luis de la Puente, Máximo Velando, and Guillermo Lobatón, the MIR was defeated militarily.

Hilda followed the events in Peru from her home in Cuba and was deeply affected by the deaths of her comrades and the MIR's misfortunes. She always thought that Luis de la Puente, who she met and got to know well in Mexico, was a born leader who would play a historical role in the revolution and was upset that he fell under such circumstances. Nevertheless, she did not believe that the guerrilla warfare was a mistake, or that the revolutionary forces had been defeated definitively.

In 1967, with Che's death in Bolivia, the era of Latin American revolutionary struggle seemed to be over. Hilda deeply suffered the loss of the partner who had shared her life in difficult circumstances in Guatemala and Mexico, the father of her daughter, and the defender of the socialist revolution on the continent. She bore great sorrow for her many fallen comrades and friends who had worked with her in Cuba. In spite of the pain, she persisted in her

---

9.   The guerrilla movement began June 9, 1965 with the taking over of the Santa Rosa mine and of several *haciendas* of the Peruvian central region.

hopes for revolution and in her commitment to the exploited disenfranchised masses.

A year later, history took a surprising turn in Peru. The Peruvian military that had defeated the MIR guerrillas deposed Belaunde in a military coup led by General Juan Velasco Alvarado on October 3, 1968.

The newly formed Revolutionary Government of the Armed Forces (FFAA), with Alvarado as president, undertook a series of nationalist measures and structural reforms. Among the main measures were the recovery of the petroleum industry, agrarian reform, state appropriation of mining companies, and the reestablishment of diplomatic relations with the socialists. The Peruvian military took partial control of the 1965 MIR guerrilla program.

Hilda had long yearned for a socialist revolution in her country. In 1969 she visited Peru and made plans to support the revolution, in which part of the left actively participated. She met with the most progressive generals and demanded a clearer definition when it came to the reestablishment of relations with Cuba and the approval of an amnesty that would allow the release of the surviving *guerrilleros* from prison. I was one of them.

Hilda decided to leave Havana and return to Peru for good, to work for the success of the revolution. She married Cuban painter Miguel Nin, who helped her settle in Lima. Hildita remained in Havana to complete high school.

When I was released in December 1970, after five years in jail, I joined Hilda in Lima. It seemed incredible that the military government had approved amnesty and pardons for the imprisoned *guerrilleros.* In this respect, the contradictions within the Armed Forces were clear. What struck me most, however, was the possibility of being at Hilda's side, after so many years and under such bewildering circumstances.

Now back in Lima, Hilda went to work, returning to her original profession. With a group of public accountants, auditors, and lawyers, Hilda advised unions and industrial communities on financial issues. She also resumed relations with progressive organizations and leftist groups in order to better understand the military process and to support the most revolutionary initiatives. For two years she lived modestly in a small apartment near Lima's Plaza de Armas.

In December 1972, during one of her trips to Havana, Hilda was involved in a car accident that caused the fracture of three of her ribs. While treating these injuries, doctors discovered that Hilda had cancer. Doctor Kourí, wife of Chancellor Raul Nibbles, operated on her. Once she recovered, she returned to Peru in her usual high spirits, to continue her projects.

In her last years in Peru, Hilda performed her duties with her typical energy and enthusiasm, but she began to perceive a certain malaise and physical deterioration. She faced her disease with courage and kept working until the end of January 1974, when she returned to Havana for medical reasons. She died shortly thereafter, in Hildita's arms.

HILDA, WHO WORKED all her life for her ideals of revolutionary transformation, would have liked to fight as Che did in the Sierra Maestra in Cuba. Like him, she directed her most noble aspirations and efforts, until her last breath, to the cause of the continent's freedom. She died in a Havana hospital, in the heart of the country she had helped to free, and where she contributed to the building of a better society.

Her obituary in *Prensa Latina* says as much:

> Today, at 2am in the morning, Monday, February 11 1974, the Peruvian revolutionary Hilda Gadea passed away. Committed to the Latin American revolutionary movement before the triumph of the Cuban Revolution, she was an ardent defender of the anti-imperialistic Guatemalan Government of Jacobo Árbenz. She is remembered for her intense activity as a militant

internationalist, the persecution she was subjected to in
Guatemala, which provoked her exile in Mexico, her active collaboration there with the *Granma* expeditionaries, with Che,
her first husband. After the Government of the Armed Forces
took power in Peru, Hilda Gadea returned to her country at
last, and divided her time between Lima and Cuba. Present at
her burial were Ramiro Valdes, member of the Political Bureau
of the Communist Party of Cuba (PCC) and Vice Prime Minister, as well as Manuel Piñeiro, Jesus Montané Oropesa and
the Commander Oscar Fernandez Mel, members of the Central Committee of the PCC.

Hilda's final resting place is in the Pantheon of the Revolutionary
Armed Forces (FAR), in the Cemetery of Havana, next to her
beloved Hildita, who died prematurely in 1995, and next to Don
Ernesto, Che's father.

TODAY IN LATIN AMERICA, the left is alive and strong again, after
the fiasco of the neoliberal tendencies of the 1980s and 1990s. Different social and political movements questioning the traditional
system of domination in the region have emerged and continue to
multiply. Some have achieved a significant representation in the
governments of several countries, as is the case in Bolivia, Ecuador,
Brazil, Argentina, Uruguay, Nicaragua, and Venezuela.

Latin America, a new world in turmoil, where the Cuban Revolution recently celebrated its forty-ninth anniversary, presents an
unprecedented landscape of popular uprisings that demand a profound change in economic, social, and political structures. And,
without a doubt, the ethical, humanist, and revolutionary example
of commander Che Guevara is still present.

In this context, full of hope, we must restore Hilda Gadea to her
deserved place in history as an honest, steadfast woman who was
able to think ahead of her times, who fought her entire life for the
revolutionary cause she had embraced when she was still very

young—a woman who contributed, like nobody else, to the ideological and political maturation of Ernesto Guevara.

—*Ricardo Gadea Acosta*
January 2008

Ricardo Gadea Acosta is Hilda's younger brother. In 1963–66, he was a member of the Central Committee of the Left Revolutionary Movement (MIR), whose best-known leaders were Luis de la Puente Uceda and Guillermo Lobatón. He was imprisoned from 1966 to 1970 for his participation in the guerrilla movement of 1965. A leftist socialist militant and leader, Acosta supported solidarity and international cooperation movements. In 1993, accused of "treason to the country" by the Fujimori administration, he was again jailed and tried by military courts but was eventually acquitted for lack of evidence. Threatened by paramilitary groups, he took refuge in Spain. Since 2002 Acosta has divided his time between Spain and Peru.

INTRODUCTION

SINCE JANUARY 1959, many reporters representing capitalist news-papers and magazines have approached me with requests for inter-views or have asked me to write about how I met Ernesto Guevara, about the period we spent together in Guatemala, and about how Che got involved in the expedition aboard the legendary boat *Granma*.

After we divorced and later still, when Che was assassinated by the soldiers of the guerilla Barrientos in Bolivia, the requests for interviews intensified. I always refused because it seemed to me a kind of exploitation. However, revolutionaries of various countries and sympathizers with the revolution all over the world were also continually asking me about these things. Moreover, a book ap-peared that requires clarification: *My Friend Che*, by Ricardo Rojo. Through his circumstantial friendship with my ex-husband and opinions based on certain publicly-known facts and controversies, Rojo arrives at conclusions that attempt to prove there was a mis-understanding between Ernesto and Fidel Castro, leader of the Cuban Revolution. These opinions, intentionally or not, aid the CIA and counterrevolutionaries with their discrediting campaigns and mark an absolute ideological rift with someone who claims to have been Che's friend.

I believe that Ernesto Guevara's life is that of an exemplary revolutionary and a man of principle, whose true understanding is essential to the struggle for justice in Latin America and in various parts of the world. For this reason, it is my duty to reveal different aspects of his life prior to his active involvement in the Latin American revolutionary process. This book does not pretend to be a complete biography, but merely a memoir of events—an account, told in the simplest way possible, of how I met Che in December 1953, and of the period that preceded his departure aboard the ship *Granma* in November 1956.

In no way am I trying to answer Rojo's allegations—Che himself has already done so in his *Diary*—but I want to establish clearly that Che's transformation into a militant revolutionary took place in Guatemala, with the attack of Yankee imperialism on that small country that was trying to consolidate a democratic government. It was there that he swore to fight for all the people of Latin America, and as a result of that decision he was included in the *Granma* expedition. Furthermore, his decision to fight for "other lands of the world" was the outcome of this conversion in Guatemala. As Che expressed it when he joined Fidel Castro's expedition—and I was a witness to this—his fight in Cuba was just one stage of his Latin American struggle.

I want to stress very clearly that when I met Ernesto Guevara in Guatemala in December 1953, he knew nothing about the Cubans who, led by Fidel Castro (at that time student leader of the Orthodox Party) had participated in the famous assault on the Moncada Barracks in Santiago, Cuba on July 26 of that year. He first learned about this from me; I talked to him about the Cubans and introduced them to him. I remember that he listened with attention and respect when I told him admiringly about the assault. However, I don't doubt that in conversation with the Argentines he may have made some ironic comment like "tell me another cowboy story," knowing Che's disposition to tease people and the Argentine habit of making everything a joke. Although Rojo said that Guevara had learned about these Cubans in San José, Costa Rica, I am in a position to testify without any doubt that Guevara first heard about the "Cubans of the 26th" from me in 1953, and it was I who introduced him to them in the beginning of January 1954 in Guatemala. As further proof, I include testimony by Myrna Torres, a Guatemalan friend, in whose house the meeting took place.

Moreover, it is fitting to point out here that Ernesto's friendship with Rojo was circumstantial. It derived from their being fellow-countrymen in a foreign land, confronted with similar economic difficulties and tackling them in the same spirit—a natural attitude of young people wanting to know the world, uniting to help each other overcome difficulties—but without entailing a deep-seated friendship or even a true ideological understanding.

Because of their particular views of Latin American problems, Guevara and Rojo had bitter arguments. Rojo was on the side of Juan José Arévalo, Victor Raúl Haya de la Torre, Victor Paz Estenssoro, and Rómulo Betancourt. Ernesto said that these men were traitors to the Latin American revolution, that they had sold out to Yankee imperialism, and that the road to follow was a different one: to fight directly against the imperialism that supported the oligarchies. Many years would pass before this approach became somewhat clear to most of our peoples, and perhaps there are still more years to go. The ideological differences between Ernesto and Rojo deepened when we learned, in Mexico after we were married, that Rojo was going to Sweden, or to another Scandinavian country, as ambassador to the Frondizi government of Argentina. Rojo came to visit us while we were on our delayed honeymoon trip to Chichén Itzá and left a letter in our apartment. On reading it, Ernesto said laughingly: "I knew *el gordo* [the chubby one] would end up compromising." I defended Rojo, suggesting that he might have done this to help in some way, but Ernesto replied: "To help? In that case, he would have stayed in Argentina, and not in any diplomatic post."

In any case, I can assert with all certainty that Che's decision to fight for the Latin American revolution in any country—including his own, Argentina—had already been made in Guatemala and was renewed when the Cuban guerrilla fights began. Rojo's suggestion that it was the alleged differences with Fidel Castro that prompted Che to leave Cuba to fight in other countries falls by its own weight.

Ernesto Guevara's life has been a model to many revolutionary leaders—Luis de la Puente, Guillermo Lobatón, Máximo Velando, Camilo Torres, Fabricio Ojeda, Javier Heraud, Juan Pablo Chang, Orlando Pantoja, Vitalio Acuña, Jesús Suárez Gayol, Coco and Inti Peredo, among others—who have pledged themselves to the struggle against exploitation, poverty, and Yankee intervention in this part of the third world. They have risked their lives in the fight against sectarianism and have called upon all true revolutionaries to participate in the struggle. Ernesto Guevara's life is an example—not only to revolutionaries, but to all men and women who feel they are truly social beings—of how one can become whole, contributing to social development, surpassing both conveniences and difficulties, even sickness, and choosing the difficult path of sacrifice.

Ernesto Guevara, with his aristocratic family background and his medical degree, could have become a favored son among the elite families in his country—he was gifted enough, intelligent, congenial, cultured. He could have been "successful" in the capitalist style: money and connections. But he eschewed those possibilities in order to contribute directly to the betterment of our lives. And later, as a minister of state and already proven as a revolutionary, he abandoned that position of power to keep on fighting for the rights of our people. Fully aware of the difficulties ahead, he knew that he could die in the effort, but that his death would not be in vain.

This account covers mainly the periods spent in Guatemala and Mexico, which I consider to have been the formative stage in Ernesto's revolutionary life. The imperialist attack on Guatemala, the people Che met—political leaders, militant revolutionaries from all the American countries, and particularly Professor Harold White—influenced him greatly. It was my privilege to have understood Ernesto's complex personality from the start, and therefore I could give him the kind of help that was within my reach: introducing him to people with whom he could discuss ideas.

It should be noted that my introducing him to Guatemalan and other political leaders—and any other steps I took to help him—were always done at his request. With that character of his, that willpower and firmness, he simply never did anything he didn't want to do, including meeting people in whom he had no interest. The only exception was during the early days of revolutionary Guatemala when our social activities often meant meeting political leaders.

Those discussions with Ernesto also of course had a great influence on me. They helped me define my anti-imperialistic conscience, and it was Ernesto who convinced me that I should stay in Guatemala, on the side of the people.

Ernesto's real personality, which had begun to emerge in Guatemala, continued of course to develop in Mexico. It grew even more during the Cuban insurrection and during his time with the revolutionary government, until he reached the greatness of a true Latin American leader with the fight in Bolivia and his message to the three continents: "two, three, many Vietnams. . . ." Throughout this latter period there was also the indubitable influence of a mutual political and ideological understanding with Fidel Castro, an influence Che acknowledged in his letter of farewell.

The essence of Che's personality I want to project herein is that of a true revolutionary who rose above himself daily, a man conscious of his limitations but who, through his own strength, was always able to give something more to society. My point is to show the basic features of Guevara the man. He is neither divine nor a myth, but a revolutionary who evolved day by day, an example for the young generations of the Americas and of the world.

Because of his faith in mankind, his love for the dispossessed, and his total commitment to the struggle against exploitation and poverty, Che renewed my hope in humankind and in the destiny of man. He showed us that only through our own effort and sacrifice shall we build a new dawn.

1

AT THE END of November 1953, I was working for the Institute for Public Works in Guatemala.

Juan Núñez Aguilar, an engineer and director of the institute, had called me and asked me to aid them in their work. I was assigned to the Department of Economic Studies. Núñez Aguilar was an influential man and a close friend of Dr. Juan José Arévalo, the former president of the republic, and of Jacobo Arbenz Guzmán, then the current president.

At the time, I was a political exile. A militant of APRA (American Popular Revolutionary Alliance), the Peruvian party of the democratic left, I was forced out of the country by the military coup led by Manuel Odría and the repression that followed. I had recently finished my studies in economics at the Major National University of San Marcos, where my militancy had led to my position in the leadership of the Youth Peruvian APRA (JAP, APRA's youth movement), representing the students.

One day Núñez Aguilar took me to meet a young Argentine lawyer, Ricardo Rojo, who had made a dramatic escape from a Buenos Aires prison during Perón's regime. In spite of my sympathies for Perón's government, for its antioligarchic measures and its support of the working class, the fact that Rojo was a political exile and a lawyer who defended political prisoners convinced me I should help him. Among the political prisoners that Rojo had defended was a Peruvian student leader, Juan Pablo Chang, who had been with me in many of the Aprista activities. Also a member of the party, he was an old friend of mine. Years later, Chang would enter the pages of Latin American history fighting side by side with Che Guevara.

Although I thought that Núñez Aguilar also sympathized with Perón's administration, he asked me to introduce Rojo into Guatemalan political circles, so that he could meet some of the Peruvian APRA leaders working in exile. We arranged an interview with two of them, Andrés Townsend Ezcurra and Nicanor Mujica. Soon thereafter, Rojo told me that he was going to Costa Rica with Walter and Domingo Beveraggi Allende, to whom he had introduced me, and that they would be joined there shortly by two other Argentines.

A month later, on December 20, Rojo introduced me to the two Argentines: Ernesto Guevara, an M.D., and Eduardo García, a lawyer. Rojo asked me to help them and explained that, since they were not political exiles, they could not obtain the official stipend that Rojo received from the Ministry of Foreign Affairs. The fact that I had a steady job and could therefore serve as a credit reference enabled me to obtain rooms for them in a boardinghouse not far from where I was living, a service I often extended to Latin Americans in exile.

Guevara and García were both in their mid-twenties, thin, and taller than the average Latin American. Guevara had dark brown hair, framing a pale face and fair features that emphasized his striking black eyes. Both were good-natured and easygoing, and Guevara had a commanding voice but a fragile appearance. His movements were agile and quick, but he gave the impression of always being relaxed. I noticed his intelligent and penetrating look and the precision of his comments. They both dressed in plain and casual clothes and nobody would have thought of them as professional men; they looked like two students. As I talked with them, I became aware that they were well educated.

On our first meeting, Guevara made a negative impression on me. He seemed superficial, egotistical, and conceited. I was more impressed by García's unaffected manner. Later, I learned that Guevara hated to ask for favors, and that at the time I met him he was suffering from an incipient attack of asthma. These attacks forced him to raise his chest in an awkward position in order to regulate his breathing. On this occasion, I remember I decided not to see the two often; they were not political exiles, so they were not brothers in our struggle, nor did we have common interests. Guevara had expressed his interest in learning what was going on in the country, and also indicated that he wanted to find work.

Two or three days later, they came to see me at the *pensión* where I lived, which was owned by Señora Anita de Toriello, a widow and a relative of the chancellor. It was located just behind the presidential palace. The Argentines talked at length about their journeys prior to their arrival in Guatemala, of their stay in Bolivia, their entry into Peru, and their meeting there with some student leaders from Lima. They showed me a card from a friend and comrade, Jorge Castro Rossmorey, in which he asked me to help them in any way I could. The card, as well as Guevara's political evaluation of the Bolivian Revolution and opinions on the Latin American reality, made me appreciate him more.

Like many Latin Americans, I tended to mistrust Argentines, first because they are often so intent on showing that their country is more developed than the rest of Latin America, and second because they have a reputation for being overconfident about their own abilities. However, I soon overcame these prejudices; not so much on account of Rojo, but rather because of the personal qualities of Guevara. A fraternal feeling had already been established in our relationship. I knew then that I was going to help him because he had something to give to society. He told me about his illness; he had suffered from asthma since he was three years old.

Thereafter, I always felt a special concern for him because of his condition.

THE FOLLOWING DAY, Gualo, as García was called, informed me that Ernesto was suffering greatly from asthma. The water and the food that he had been eating at the house of some Venezuelans had brought about the attack. Gualo came to pick me up and together we went to Ernesto's house. He was reading when we arrived; the worst part of the attack was over. That evening they told me about the last stage of their journey—Costa Rica.

Guevara told me that he had met Rómulo Betancourt and Juan Bosch; both these men would later become presidents of their respective countries. Ernesto considered Betancourt's political position plainly dishonest and related a conversation they had had in which Betancourt was very unclear as to his stance on the Yankee penetration of Latin America. He told me that he had asked Betancourt directly: "In case of war, which side would you be on, that of the Soviet Union or the United States?" Betancourt's answer had been: "On the side of the United States, of course." That definitely qualified Betancourt as a traitor. "You will see," Ernesto said, "he will rise to power and will betray his people; more and more he will surrender his country to the imperialists."

He then told me how he had visited Venezuela during his first trip, a country where there was only oil, no industry, and where agriculture was developed to a minimal degree. Everything was imported from the United States, even lettuce, eggs, and chickens— he had checked this at the market in Caracas. The position of Betancourt, he went on to say, was the same as that of Haya de la Torre, Figueres, and Paz Estenssoro: "They all represent complete submission to imperialism; they are afraid to seek the support of the people to fight it." Time would prove him right.

He told me that he had come to Guatemala from La Paz, where he had met Rojo. His original plan had been to go to

Venezuela, where he was to meet his longtime friend Alberto Granados; he already had a job there that would pay eight hundred dollars a month. He decided in La Paz that his real interest was in learning as much as possible about the revolution in Latin America, and that the pursuit of this goal would leave him no time to earn money. Furthermore, he wanted a deeper knowledge of the Latin American countries and had decided to remain in Latin America for the next ten years, after which he planned to go back to Argentina. He wanted also to visit Europe and, being an Argentine, he wanted to go to Paris. I teased him about this, saying that what he really wanted to see was the Parisian cafés and the bohemian life of the Left Bank. I advised him to read José Carlos Mariátegui to learn how to study Europe. We talked about Mariátegui's works, *El alma matinal* and *Seven Essays on the Peruvian Reality*.

I am reminded of an incident from those days that revealed some aspects of Guevara's personality. He had, I found, an acute psychological perceptiveness, which enabled him to understand people. Gualo said to him at one point: "*Querido*, that's not the way it is . . ." This expression, "dear," used between men is common in Argentina, but at that time I was not familiar with it and I found the term ambiguous, like everything the Argentines said. I said nothing and tried to hide my distaste for the term. Guevara, however, protested: "Gualo, you know that I don't like it when you call me *querido*. People who do not understand our way of speaking may think strange things. . . ."

It was about that time that I decided to introduce them not only to political exiles but also to my other personal friends. In addition to the few, select guests of the Pensión Toriello, where I lived, I was a good friend of Myrna Torres and her family. Her father, Professor Edelberto Torres, was an exile from Nicaragua; he was well respected in Guatemalan cultural circles and among the different exile groups. He was a scholar, and a fervent admirer of the great poet Rubén Darío. His family was charming: his wife, Doña Marta, an amiable and active housewife, and his three children, Edelberto, Myrna, and Grazia. I had met Professor Torres at many of the political and cultural meetings in which exiles participated, but the fact that his daughter Myrna worked in the same place as I deepened my friendship with the family. Myrna was a bilingual secretary in the credit department; she was a restless, happy girl, full of sympathy and charm, and we quickly became friends. She liked me immediately because I was South American and because I was a political exile. She took me to her home, where I was very well received. Soon I was treated as one of their children and I became friends with all the family circle; they were all revolutionaries, some of them members of the Communist Youth Alliance. We attended their meetings, parties, and picnics and from time to time we went to revolutionary concerts and events.

2

THE FIGHTERS WHO had attacked the Moncada Barracks in Cuba
and taken asylum in the Guatemalan embassy in Havana arrived in
the country in September 1953. They were Antonio "Ñico" López,
Mario Dalmau, Armando Arencibia, and Antonio Darío López,
"El Gallego." The assault on the barracks on July 26 had caught
my attention at the time. When I heard of the participants' arrival
I asked Edmundo Guerra, a revolutionary comrade, to introduce
me to them. I wanted to find out from them who Fidel Castro was,
how the attack had been organized, why it failed, and what their
goals had been.

At this time Guatemala was engaged in revolution, and it had
become a refuge for many Latin American political exiles. My closest friends were the Peruvian exiles from APRA, Andrés Townsend
Ezcurra, Nicanor Mujica, Hipólito Alfaro and his wife, Blanca; José
Russo and his wife, Teresa; Jorge Raygada; Ricardo Temoche and
his wife; and Carlos Malpica and his children among them. I also
had friends among the exiles from Venezuela, Nicaragua, and Honduras, as well as some Chilean technicians working in Guatemala.
The majority of them had left by the time the Argentines and the
Cubans arrived; only the Townsends, the Mujicas, the Temoches,
and the Alfaros were still in the country.

The Cuban exiles from the Moncada were quite different from
the others. They were a very lively group. They had hardly any political indoctrination—almost all of them were workers—yet they

boasted the short but outstanding accomplishment of the Moncada attack. Ñico was noticeable not only on account of his tall and slender figure, but also because of his deep conviction that one had to make a revolution, and that in Cuba this revolution was going to be made by Fidel. Ñico told me about Fidel's career as a student leader, about his militance in the Orthodox Party of Chíbas; about how Fidel had gotten the students to support the government of Prío Socarrás after Fulgencio Batista staged a coup on March 10, 1952, despite considering Prío a political enemy. Ñico told me how, after Batista's coup, Fidel saw very clearly the necessity for the struggle and that when the party refused to accept his point of view, Fidel formed a group made up mostly of workers, clerks, and students. When I asked him how they had organized the attack while keeping it secret, he answered that it was all due to Fidel's good leadership. He expressed his faith in his leader with great enthusiasm, concluding: "Fidel is the greatest and most honest man born in Cuba since Martí. He will make the revolution." History would prove him right.

I also learned from Ñico how they had met and agreed on decisions and how later on they had begun training with only two or three firearms. To fund the movement, they sold whatever they had, their automobiles and even their jobs. Having put together a little money, they began launching their operations. One day Fidel had asked them to meet, and to be prepared to leave Havana after the meeting. They were not told their final destination. They traveled to Santiago de Cuba and from there to Siboney Farm, where the final plans were revealed to them. The goal was to attack and seize the Moncada army headquarters; they were given the date, time, and details. Ñico told me how, during the action, two groups of attackers made mistakes: one group withdrew unexpectedly, and another group, not recognizing their own people, began to attack them. Few succeeded in breaking through the ring of police. Afterward a few took asylum in the Guatemalan embassy; many were massacred.

Fidel and a few others, including Haydée Santamaría and Melba Hernández, who were acting as nurses, were taken prisoner.

Ñico was sure that his stay in Guatemala would be a short one and that soon he would be leaving for another country to join Fidel and work for the revolution. His faith was so great that whoever listened to him would believe him.

The Moncada attack revealed a new technique. Like other revolutionaries, I am convinced that the real problem is tactical: how to take power so that we will be able to carry out the adequate transformation and creation of a just society. This is what we exiles talked about all the time, and it was also the reason for the great respect we had for the Guatemalan Revolution. However, we saw our entire Latin American continent in the hands of the oligarchies, and we knew that each time a democratic option opened up, no matter how feeble, the ruling classes would stage a coup to end all possibilities of real change. After the Bolivian Revolution of April 1952 came the Moncada action on July 26, 1953, a hopeful sign in the Latin American political scene. In my opinion, both tactics and strategy had changed: to capture an army headquarters in a nearby mountainous area seemed to be the way to continue the fighting in the mountains. When I asked Ñico about this, he answered that he could not reveal plans for the future, and he limited himself to saying that the action was meant to be only the spark of the revolution.

At any rate, the fact that Ñico and his comrades had taken part in that action produced a certain respect on the part of the rest of the exiles, particularly toward Ñico himself, whose awareness was greater. He became the closest of my Cuban friends. He knew about the Apristas' admiration for Cuban politician Eduardo Chíbas and told me that they had a Cuban Aprista Party with offices in the same building as those of the Orthodox Party.

Soon after I had introduced the Cubans to Myrna and her friends, they became part of the group, and because of their spirit and enthusiasm they were included in everything political—meetings, parties, and picnics.

Their arrival had been preceded by that of another Cuban, Benjamín de Yurre (a member of Prío Socarrás's group), who was also an exile. Through Yurre we met Harold White, a North American professor who, after several years of research, had written a book on Marxism. Both these men became members of our group. Our meetings were a joy to me; there were no alcoholic beverages and we never had problems of any kind. When the Argentines arrived, Yurre had already gone to Miami to join his group, but White remained.

At the close of 1953, both Guevara and Gualo García were already close friends of mine. They often came to visit and I went to concerts and political meetings with them. Clouds were already gathering on the Guatemalan horizon; the imperialists had started a frontal attack on the nationalization of the lands previously owned by the United Fruit Company, whose board of directors included Allen Dulles.

Ernesto and I discussed at length the Bolivian Revolution, in which all revolutionaries saw hope. As a member of the APRA Party, my sympathies were with Paz Estenssoro, whose intellectual capacity and revolutionary pronouncements I admired. Guevara, however, felt that this was not a true revolution, that the leadership was corrupt and consequently would end up surrendering to Yankee imperialism. At that time my faith in the Bolivian Revolution led me to argue that we were talking about a small country, without a coast and consequently limited, and with only one resource, tin. I went on to argue that with the wise development of other natural resources Bolivia could achieve its economic independence. At the same time, I had to admit that for the moment, Bolivia could only find consumers for its tin in the traditional market for Latin America: the United States. Sometimes our discussions would get heated. Ernesto maintained that the Soviet Union could absorb this production and provide economic help for the installment of a refining plant that would allow Bolivia to sell not only refined tin but other manufactured products. Although I saw the logic in his argument, I thought this solution too daring for the moment. Whenever Rojo joined our discussions, they ended in near fights, and I would try to close the conversation by stating that theory was one thing and practice was another; that, once in power, things might look different; and that he, Rojo, did not have the right to talk since he had done nothing to change the situation in his own country. I said that a social problem is not a chemical laboratory, where one can combine some elements and produce others. It is much more difficult: one should take into account not only the social structure and class division, but also the different degrees of economic development in specific regions and the level of individual development. Argentina, I would say, was different from Bolivia, Peru, or Guatemala, where a large part of the population was Indian. These people retained their customs; they were not integrated into the economic system of the West but only suffered its repercussions. Ernesto understood these arguments; his love of archaeology had taken him into the indigenous cultures of America, and he already knew something about the Inca, Maya, and Aztec societies. However, the main issue in our discussion of the Bolivian Revolution was never settled between us. History would prove him right.

One day I introduced Rojo and Guevara to a very good friend, an exile from Honduras. She was a charming woman with a profound knowledge of Marxism and a leading position in the Alliance of Women, and had been in the Soviet Union and in China. Her name was Elena Leiva de Holst, and she was like a mother to me. I used to spend many a Sunday at her house.

Elena was married to a German businessman, whom I also liked very much. Henry Holst enjoyed many talks with Guevara and Rojo, and during these discussions Guevara would talk about his great admiration of the achievements of the revolution in the

Soviet Union, while Rojo and I frequently interposed objections. Mine were not regarding the theory behind these achievements but rather the practices, since they could not be transplanted intact or without change into our very different realities. But I sympathized with the revolution, while Rojo deprecated it with superficial arguments. Once, after one of these conversations, while they were taking me home, the discussion started again and promptly became bitter. The subject was the same as always. The only path, said Ernesto, was a violent revolution; the struggle had to be against Yankee imperialism and any other solutions, such as those offered by APRA, Democratic Action, the National Revolutionary Movement of Bolivia (MNR), were betrayals. Rojo countered that the electoral process did offer a solution. The discussion became more heated with each argument offered. I abstained; I was becoming more convinced each day that no election was going to give our people power. I did try to quiet Guevara a little, but he reacted brusquely. "I don't want anybody to calm me down!" he almost shouted. I was stunned by the realization that it was no longer possible to argue with him. I decided then not to speak to him anymore.

He must have realized what had happened, because on the bus on the way home he apologized: "Forgive me. I get carried away with the discussion and I do not realize what I say. None of what happened is your fault; it is just that this fat fellow with his arguments for surrender makes me lose my mind. He will end up as an agent of imperialism." I accepted his apology and added that I did not believe Rojo would sell out to the Yankees.

Once again Ernesto expressed his wish to get a job, so I introduced him to several Guatemalan officials who were my friends: Alfonso Bauer Paiz, minister of economy, Jaime Díaz Rozzoto, secretary of the presidency, and Marco Antonio Villamar, a congressman. They all asked us to visit them in their homes, and in each case a friendship developed with Ernesto, who was very eager to find out from them about the problems of the Guatemalan Revolution. He also informed them of his desire to work in Petén, the country's jungle area.

All the people we knew agreed that he would have to speak to the minister of public health to get the job he wanted. Finally, through a Venezuelan doctor also in exile, Dr. Peñalver, he was able to obtain an interview with the minister. He was informed by the minister that his diploma had to be revalidated, and that this would require going to medical school for a year. Ernesto abandoned the idea of working in Petén, but he wanted to remain in Guatemala for another year, so a job was indispensable. He was willing to work as a nurse or whatever he could get. He had accompanied Dr. Peñalver on his visits to some of the province towns, going all the way to Quiriguá, in Petén, where there were some ruins from the ancient Maya civilization.

Ernesto asked me to introduce him to José Manuel Fortuny, secretary-general of the Guatemalan Party of Labor, PGT, with whom he wanted to talk about agrarian reform. In spite of my insistence, Fortuny never granted the interview. Years later, when the Cuban Revolution was in power, Fortuny wrote Guevara from exile saying that he wanted to go to Cuba. Ernesto authorized the visa and gave him a job.

3

ERNESTO'S VISITS TO my house became a daily event. He would tell me about his trips in Latin America with Alberto Granados ("Shorty"), as he called him, and "Calica" Ferrer. He told me how he had arrived in the United States in an airplane chartered by an uncle of his who sold horses in the north. He had made two trips to Peru, two to Venezuela, one to Chile, and one to Bolivia. He went from Bolivia to Peru on a second visit and then on to Ecuador, Panama, Costa Rica, and Guatemala. He told me that the second trip to Chile was on a motorcycle, with Shorty, and that when the motorcycle broke down they were forced to continue their journey by foot. They stopped at the mines of Chuquicamata, where they saw the subhuman conditions in which the Chilean miners lived and the courage with which they endured their lives. "However," he emphasized, "if those miners had good leaders, they could make a revolution and take power; they are courageous and they could not be any poorer."

He told me about his first visit to Machu Picchu and the marvels of these great pre-Inca ruins. From Machu Picchu they continued to a leprosarium in a little town in the jungle. Ernesto had a letter from a Peruvian doctor, Hugo Pesce, whom he knew and admired from the lengthy conversations they had had; it was a letter of introduction to the leprosarium, and it opened the doors of this institution for them. Whereas the other doctors diminished the human dignity of the patients, Ernesto and Granados dealt with them without any qualms; they did not wear masks or gloves and they looked the patients in the face. Ernesto and Granados treated them as equals. They even played football with them—and the patients loved them. Whenever Ernesto referred to them, it was with respect and affection. He used to comment on how patients without hope were always the most generous in their relations with other patients. It was the patients of this leprosarium who built the raft *Mambo-Tango*, in which Ernesto and Granados continued their trip. There was a farewell party for them given by the patients and the staff. From here they went through the Amazon country up to Colombia, where they took a plane to Venezuela.

Granados remained to work in Caracas, and Ernesto went to Miami in the air transport for horses. He stayed with a friend, living on hot dogs and pursuing his inveterate habit of striking up conversations, despite his rudimentary English, with anyone and everyone. Perhaps during one of these conversations, somebody from the FBI heard him venting his anti-Yankee attitudes. In any case, he was arrested, questioned, and sent back to Argentina. Ernesto had wanted to go back anyway; he had twelve more courses to take before graduating. He spent the next six months in school, finishing his medical studies.

After graduating, he embarked on a journey. This time he planned to be gone ten years. He repeated this to me often, and later, in the first letter he wrote to my parents, he again mentioned that he planned to be away from his country for ten years. This time he and Calica Ferrer took a third-class car on the Buenos Aires–La Paz railroad. During the trip, they had occasion to see the northwest of Argentina and many small provincial towns of Bolivia. In Bolivia, he met Juan Lechín Oquendo, Nuflo Chaves, and other leaders. His general impression of Bolivia was negative; he saw the extreme poverty of the people, the weak measures the revolution took in the nationalization of the mines, and the lack of respect for the peasants on the part of the government. He also saw opportunism and corruption in many officials. From Bolivia he went to Peru, traveling with Ricardo Rojo and Calica Ferrer in a truck loaded with peasants. In Puno, a border town between Peru and Bolivia, the Peruvian police confiscated all the Bolivian books he had with him. From there they went to Cuzco, and again to Machu Picchu, where he met a German photographer who took many interesting photographs that later became part of an article Ernesto wrote on Machu Picchu. Thence they went to Lima by bus, where Ernesto checked in with the police but did not get his Bolivian books back. In Lima he met Gualo García, and together they visited the home of a leftist nurse. In her house they met with several Aprista leaders, among them Castro Rossmorey. It was he who gave them a card for me when they told him that they were headed for Guatemala. He also went to visit Dr. Pesce, who was delighted to receive him and they spent much time in conversation. Later, when he asked me if I knew Pesce, I said I didn't know him personally, but I did know that he was a scientist of prestige, connected with the Communist Party.

Calica Ferrer returned to Argentina, and Ernesto and Gualo left for Ecuador. In Ecuador they met Rojo again. They also met with many leaders from the Communist Youth and some intellectuals. They had a long conversation with Jorge Icaza on the condition of the peasants in Ecuador; and he autographed his book *Huasipungo* for Ernesto. Years later, Ernesto gave me this book.

Their next stop was Panama, and again there were many conversations with student leaders. His visit to the Canal Zone again roused his indignation for Yankee imperialism. When he spoke to me about this, he said that the original position taken by APRA on this question was good, but that Haya de la Torre had betrayed it later.

In order to pay for plane fare to Costa Rica, Ernesto had to pawn all of his medical books. He told me that he subsequently tried to recover them, writing to a Panamanian student, a comrade, to ask him to get the books. He never received an answer, but years later in Cuba, a Panamanian leader told me someone had the books and wanted to know how he could return them. I indicated a way but don't know if they ever were sent.

From Costa Rica, Ernesto and Gualo continued to Guatemala on foot. One day, walking in a heavy rain, they stopped an automobile and to their surprise found Rojo and the Beveraggi Allende brothers in it. From there, they traveled with them all the way to Guatemala City. During the last part of this trip, he met Carlos Luis Fallas, who gave Ernesto his book *Mamita Yunai.*

ERNESTO TOLD ME about his childhood. Born in Rosario to parents from Buenos Aires, the whole family had to move to Córdoba on account of his illness—he had been afflicted with asthma from the time he was three years old. The wealth of this aristocratic family had shrunk steadily due to his father's unfortunate investments and his refusal to exploit his workers. First he had a maté plantation on the Paraguayan border, later a shipyard for small yachts, followed by a variety of other businesses.

Ernesto told me also about his childhood friends and his adolescence; about his girlfriend in Córdoba, Chichina Ferreira, whom he loved but could not marry as he knew that he would not be able to live chained down in a provincial town. He wanted to walk the world and return to his country after ten years. He told me about his family in detail: his parents, brothers, and sisters. Whenever he spoke of them it was with warmth and affection. His tie with his mother was very deep, he said: "The old lady liked to go around with a bunch of intellectual women; they may turn out to be lesbians." But there was always a tone of admiration and deep affection for the "old lady," a term, he explained, that the Argentines use for parents.

It was his love for his family that made me appreciate Ernesto's humanity: he was generous and tender despite of his outward cynicism and irony toward his family and himself. However, what impressed me more was his attitude as a newly graduated doctor. His judgment in relation to the malnutrition, extreme poverty, and filth in which the majority of our people live was wise, enriched by the experience of his travels through Latin America. I will always remember the time we discussed A. J. Cronin's *The Citadel* and other books dealing with the subject. Ernesto insisted that doctors in our countries should not be pampered professionals, taking care of only the privileged classes: inventing remedies, prescribing useless medicines, performing unnecessary operations for imaginary diseases, or for curing illnesses resulting from an idle life or from the frivolous or exaggerated satisfaction of vital needs. Of course, he said, this path leads to high income and a "successful" life, but this must not be the goal of any young professional aware of the needs of our nations. He told me that he could have remained in the allergy clinic of Dr. Pisani; he had already worked a year there. His own infirmity, a family illness, had made him decide to specialize in allergies. But he did not want to become a well-paid doctor of the bourgeoisie.

One time he showed me something he was writing on the role of a doctor in the different countries of Latin America. It analyzed the lack of state protection and the scarcity of resources facing the medical profession, as well as the tremendous sanitation problems prevailing in our countries. His work was a compilation of data with brief comments, but he kept developing it. The original work got lost on one of his trips, but at the time that he showed it to me it was already sixty pages long. He asked me to help him collect health statistics for each Latin American country, and I promised to do so, as I believed it a very worthwhile work. Moreover, it showed me that this was the work of a restless mind, sensitive to social problems. I knew then that this quality would lead him to a political militancy that was more advanced than the theoretical position he already held.

All of this led him to analyze the governmental system of each nation in our continent and the degree of its exploitation by the local oligarchies and Yankee imperialism. Frequently, this ended in an analysis of what we had read about what was being done in the Soviet Union. The affinity in our reading helped us better understand each other and gave us fodder for our interminable conversations.

We had both read all the pre-revolution Russian novels: Tolstoy, Gorky, Dostoyevsky, Kropotkin's *Memoirs of a Revolutionist.* Later our discussions covered such works as: *What to Do?, Imperialism, Final Stage of Capitalism, Anti-Dühring, The Communist Manifesto, The Origin of the Family, Private Property and the State,* and other works by Lenin, Marx, and Engels. We also discussed Engels' *Landmarks of Scientific Socialism* and Marx's *Das Kapital,* works with which I was more familiar due to my studies in economics.

As for general culture, we had read more or less the same books; the classics, the modern novels, and some novels on adventures and space travel. Laughing, Ernesto told me how when he was still in high school he decided to start reading seriously and began by swallowing his father's library, choosing volumes at random. The books were not classified; next to an adventure book he would find a Greek tragedy and then a book on Marxism. His political activities, he told me, involved attending anti-Perón meetings with his father; and during his university days, after a short time in the organization, he decided to leave the Communist Youth because he felt the Communists were getting away from the people. He had left Argentina to avoid military service in the navy, and while he was away he understood that Perón had begun a struggle against the oligarchy and against imperialism, introducing laws to protect the workers.

Although I didn't like certain fascist aspects of Perón's regime, I had to admit that in general it was a government that stood for popular causes. I particularly disliked the propaganda and the methods the government was using in education. I knew well the attacks against the Federation of Argentine Universities from my time as a student leader.

I told Ernesto about the Chinese Revolution and lent him Mao Tse-tung's *New China*. It was the first work he had read on the great revolution. When he finished reading it, we talked about the book, and he expressed great admiration for the long struggle of the Chinese people to take power with the help of the Soviet Union. He also understood that their road toward socialism was somewhat different from the one followed by the Soviets and that the Chinese reality was closer to that of our Indians and peasants. Since I also admired the Chinese Revolution, we often talked about it and about what was being done there.

Later he suggested that we go to China together. Seeing my surprise, he formally promised not to court me and added: "When I promise something, I keep my promise." His behavior afterward would confirm his statement and give me faith in him, despite of my skepticism. However, my reaction wasn't exactly caused by what he thought; rather, it was the fact that I wasn't used to making travel plans in such haste. I thought about his attitude and concluded that it was good. I told him that one could not go to China as a regular tourist; it was necessary to first establish a contact in order to be included in one of the periodic tours, and that payment of part of the passage was required. We agreed that we would explore the possibilities of going there together.

By that time, Guevara and García had met Peruvian exiles at the house of some Venezuelan exiles and the two also knew Myrna and her family. I wanted to introduce them to the Cubans. I had already talked to Ernesto about Ñico and he expressed interest in meeting him. It was the end of the year; Myrna, with her unending enthusiasm that was comparable only to that of Ñico, planned a party at her house for the evening of December 31. The party was to take place after a costume parade organized by Ñico, and for which he had obtained a truck. We were to wear costumes and ride the truck along Sixth Avenue, much in the style of the Paseo del Prado in Havana during the carnivals. Ñico's idea was immediately taken up by Myrna. But New Year's Eve always made me sad and I had no wish to participate. I knew I would be thinking about my family. I didn't go with them to the parade, but I did go to the party. The Argentines didn't come—they were at another gathering at the Venezuelans'—and I missed Ernesto somewhat, since he was the only one with whom I could talk about serious subjects. The Cubans were disappointed when the Argentines did not show up, but in general it was a good party and for a few hours we forgot all our troubles.

4

THE CHIEF OF the Aprista Party, Víctor Raúl Haya de la Torre, had taken asylum in the Colombian embassy in Lima, and in January 1954 we heard that he had been granted a travel permit and that he was going to pass through Guatemala on his way to Mexico. He would be at the airport only a few hours. This news traveled fast throughout Guatemala's political circles, but I was still very surprised when Ernesto called to ask me to bring him along if I was going to the airport. He said he very much wanted to meet Haya de la Torre. "How can that be?" I asked. "You don't believe he is still a revolutionary, do you?"

"Precisely because I don't. I would very much like to ask him a couple of questions about Latin American relations with the U.S. I want to remind you that I have talked with Betancourt."

I said that if the invitation depended on me there would be no problem. Unfortunately, I wasn't able to arrange it: the Peruvian exiles wanted to use the short time available to talk to Haya de la Torre. Also, the automobile in which I traveled to the airport had no room for more people.

I was the only representative of the left wing of APRA, because the rest of my comrades were no longer in Guatemala. I wanted to ask Haya de la Torre not to go to the United States, and to tell him that if he went it would be of disastrous consequences for APRA internally. People would be very confused; they would not be able to reconcile an anti-imperialist position with any form of support from the United States. In the end, I wasn't able to talk with Haya de la Torre, but I gave him a letter stating my point of view. This was done, of course, without consulting or telling anyone in the Party about it.

Later, in talking about it with Ernesto, who knew nothing about my plans, he asked: "But . . . did you explain your doubts?"

"I couldn't," I answered. "He gave me the impression he was very tired. But mostly he was surrounded by others and it was impossible to talk to him." Then I told Ernesto about the letter. He laughed skeptically and said: "You will see; he won't even answer. Anyhow, I would have liked to ask him what I asked Betancourt. I am sure his answer would have been the same."

I had a presentiment that he was right. A few days later we read Haya de la Torre's article for *Life* magazine, in which he narrated his five years in exile. Everyone knew that he was paid very well for this article.

ONE DAY IN early January, I introduced the Cubans to Ernesto and Gualo. They liked each other immediately. On that day Ernesto heard a firsthand account of the attack on the Moncada. This was a good start for a friendship between Ñico and Ernesto. The Cubans were good boys; although they weren't very strong in theory, they were good and sincere fighters. They had done something concrete, for which respect was due. I relayed to Ernesto all that Ñico had told me about the Moncada attack and about Fidel.

The Argentines were very well liked by Myrna and her family, especially by Edelberto Torres, who immediately recognized Ernesto's hunger for knowledge. He showed vivid interest in learning about the Chinese Revolution from Don Edelberto, who had been there. The first time I took García, Guevara, and Rojo to the Torres home, Myrna had put a well-known tango on the record player and had insisted that the Argentines dance. Guevara asked me to dance with him. I did and was greatly disappointed when I discovered that he could hardly dance a step; I had to use all of my self-control not to quit before the record was over. He laughed and meekly apologized. If he wasn't a good dancer, at least he could talk about anything—politics, philosophy, art, and so on—so it was easy to excuse him, and we both laughed at his lack of rhythm. He proceeded to tell me some anecdotes about his lack of musicality, and later on, when we were married, I had plenty of opportunity to learn just how right he was.

Ernesto became a very good friend of the Cubans and we saw them often at parties and picnics. One particular picnic comes to mind. We were in the country home of a German businessman. There were Rojo, García, Guevara, Oscar Valdovinos and his Panamanian wife, Myrna, with several friends, Ñico with the other Cubans, and a friend from Honduras who played the accordion. We spent a wonderful day there; we took pictures, went horseback riding—I had a chance to admire Ernesto's expert handling of the horse—ate hot dogs and baked potatoes, and at sundown we built a fire, sat around it, and listened to the Honduran play Viennese waltzes.

As we were walking through the fields, Guevara caught up with me, and to my surprise, without any preamble, asked me: "Are you completely healthy? Is your family in good health?" I looked at him, trying to find an answer, and then I laughed. "Are you writing my clinical history?" I asked, and after a moment, added seriously: "Yes, I am very healthy, and so is my entire family. Why are you asking me such things?" I added mockingly: "Is your interest entirely professional or are you perhaps going to propose?" He smiled "Maybe it's not a bad idea. . . . What do you think?" I answered: "We'll see. It's too soon to tell."

Until he asked me about my health, I had not realized the problem that his chronic asthma represented for him. It must be complicated, I thought, to be married to a person with such a condition; children are likely to inherit the disease.

A long time would go by before I came to grips seriously with the problem he had brought up so lightly. As a girl from Lima accustomed to joking, and a skeptic as well, I was going to be very difficult to convince. And so it was: not until January 1955 did I answer definitely. And then it was almost by chance, not because I planned it. In fact, if I had not been deported from Guatemala to Mexico, we wouldn't have met again.

Another day we went to the university's swimming pool with Rojo, García, Señora Temoche and a North American couple, a professor of economics from Rutgers University, Robert Alexander and his wife. They had been introduced to me by Harry Kantor, another North American professor, a specialist on Peru and a friend of APRA. Later, Consuelo España, the sister-in-law of Alfonso Bauer Paiz, joined us. There wasn't the usual heated discussion that day; Professor Alexander asked about different aspects of the Guatemalan Revolution and wrote down some of the answers he received. Later, when Ernesto, who didn't like North Americans, took me home, he asked: "Are you sure they're not spies? I see many gringos around here." It was true; there were many North American visitors. Perhaps some of them were taking down information for the CIA, but many of them were sincerely interested in learning about Guatemala, its history, and its revolution.

ONE DAY ERNESTO and Gualo came to the boardinghouse where I lived to ask me for a loan of fifty dollars, which they needed to pay their room and board. They said they would return the money once they were working. I mentioned that I was surprised they hadn't borrowed from Rojo; Guevara replied that he did not like to ask him. Unfortunately, although I was making a good salary, I was sending money to Peru every month and I didn't have the money to lend them. I showed the receipt for a money order I had just sent. However, I did want to help, so I gave them two pieces of jewelry, a gold medal on a chain and a gold ring. I told them that

I didn't use those pieces and that they could pawn them and re-deem them sometime if they had the money, but that I didn't re-ally need them.

They were grateful and thanked me. I responded that I wasn't doing anything out of the ordinary. Later, they were both working with the Cubans, selling cheap articles in the provinces, but never made enough money to have any left after paying for the essentials.

ON FEBRUARY 18, Rojo and García came to my office, and Guevara with them. They came to tell me that they were leaving the coun-try. Rojo was going to the United States; García was returning to Argentina. He was thinking of getting married and settling down. He said he was tired of traveling.

Guevara was suffering that day from an asthma attack. He tried to hide it but his breathing was difficult. He replied to my in-quiry "How are you?" with a typical Argentine brusqueness that left me a little annoyed. Rojo noticed it and said: "We will leave you two alone to find some mutual sympathy." He and García left to go say goodbye to the president of the institute. Months later Ernesto informed me that they used to tease him about me and my interest in him, although up to that point it had been only intel-lectual and political. But it's true that I had a special consideration for Guevara because of his asthma. Rojo's comment had embar-rassed me and to cover it up, I asked Ernesto what he was doing. He said he was reading some books on Guatemala that the Venezue-lan had lent him, and soon we were exchanging views on other works—on the *Popol Vuh*, which is the classic "creation story" of the ancient Quiché Mayans; on Miguel Angel Asturias' *El Señor Pres-idente;* Landívar's poetry; José Milla's *Canasto del sastre;* and Luis Cardoza y Aragón's *Retorno al futuro* and *Pequeña sinfonía del Nuevo Mundo.*

Soon Rojo and García returned; they said goodbye and asked me to help Ernesto since he was going to be alone and to introduce him to people in the Health Department, where he might get a job.

By this time almost all of the Peruvian and Venezuelan exiles had departed. One could see a coup in the offing. At the end of January, President Arbenz had denounced an imminent armed invasion supported by "a government to the north." In spite of the denial by the U.S. State Department—which claimed that the charge was aimed at undermining the Tenth International Conference to be held in March—everyone knew that the invasion was a sham to condemn Guatemala and its efforts as being "Communist." The Guatemalan government had dared to expropriate large landholdings, including property of the United Fruit Company.

Rojo had also realized this and left. Ernesto and I discussed the matter at length. We decided to stay and see if the United States really supported a direct attack and if the Guatemalan democracy could defend itself. We decided to be on the side of Guatemala.

Ernesto called on February 21 and asked me to accompany him to a political rally in commemoration of the assassination of Augusto César Sandino, the Nicaraguan guerrilla leader. I accepted the invitation. When he called for me, I was surprised to see him dressed in a gray business suit. "I inherited it from Gualo," he explained. He looked very nice. It was the first time I had seen him in a suit; he usually wore casual clothes. He always did his own washing, and he told me that he preferred nylon because it was much easier to care for, especially when traveling.

Up to that moment, I had not realized how simply he dressed and how unconcerned he was about clothes; his personality made such details inconsequential. Little by little it became clear that this was his way of deprecating material possessions.

On this occasion he made an observation that revealed another aspect of his personality. Present at the rally was a high Guatemalan official whom we had met. He was in the company of a very beautiful woman, a young starlet. We knew that he was married. Ernesto asked: "Why is he going around with another woman?" I answered: "Apparently he's having problems with his wife."

"Well," he said, "if they told me he was leaving his wife for somebody like you, a thinking woman, that would be all right; but to change one pretty face for another, for a man like him, a politician with other values, makes no sense."

I was surprised at his reference to me and I turned to look at him, but he had "meant what he said": it was the way he thought.

Two days later, Ernesto called me at the office to tell me that he hadn't been able to come to see me the day before because he had been ill, and that the asthma attack would last several days. I promised to stop by to see him after work. Accordingly, around six o'clock in the evening, I arrived at his boardinghouse on Fifth Street. His room was upstairs, but despite of his illness he was waiting for me in the downstairs hall. It was the first time I had seen him or anyone else suffering from an acute attack of asthma, and I was shocked by the tremendous difficulty he had in breathing and by the deep wheeze that came from his chest. I hid my concern but insisted that he lie down. He agreed that it would be better, but he couldn't climb the stairs and refused to accept my help. He told me where his room was and asked me to go up and bring him a syringe and a bottle of liquid, both of which were on his night table, along with a bottle of alcohol and cotton swabs. I did as he asked and watched him as he applied an injection of Adrenalin.

He rested a bit and began to breathe more easily. We went slowly up the stairs; we reached his room and he lay down. He told me that since the age of ten he had been able to give himself injections. It was in that moment that I came to a full realization of what his illness meant. I couldn't help but admire his strength of character and his self-discipline. His dinner was brought up: boiled rice and fruit. "That's all," he said. He had to eat simple fare in order to get rid of the toxins that he had accumulated going around to the many farewell parties with Rojo.

Trying to conceal how much I had been touched by all this, I talked about everything and anything, all the while thinking what a shame it was that a man of such value who could do so much for society, so intelligent and so generous, had to suffer such an affliction; if I were in his place I would shoot myself. I decided right there to stick by him, without, of course, getting involved emotionally. I remember I concluded at that time, as he talked to me about his mother, that his strength of character must have come from her. (I was right; all his subsequent conversation about her confirmed it.) For the next two or three days I visited him after work. His condition improved, thanks to the injections and the light diet. During these visits he explained what an allergy was. He told me of the recent experiments that were being carried out in Dr. Pisani's clinic with semidigested foods; and of how everyone in his family suffered from allergies. According to him the illness was hereditary, passed along by his mother's family.

I discovered that he liked poetry. I gave him a book of poems by César Vallejo and other poems published in Guatemala at that time. I remember a poem entitled "Tu Nombre," which had appeared in the newspaper. Two days after I gave it to him, he recited it for me. Not that I took it personally; I am merely expressing my admiration for his ability to memorize. Ernesto had a wide knowledge of Latin American poetry and could easily recite any poem by Pablo Neruda, whom he admired greatly. Among his favorite poets were Federico García Lorca, Miguel Hernández, Machado, Gabriela Mistral, César Vallejo; a few Argentines like José Hernández, whose "Martín Fierro" he could recite completely from memory; Jorge Luis Borges, Leopoldo Marechal, Alfonsina Storni, and the Uruguayans Juana de Ibarborou and Sara de Ibáñez. In particular he loved Ibáñez, to whose work I had introduced him. He considered her the best postmodernist woman poet, and I agreed with him. He used to recite "Los Palídos," "Pasión y Muerte de la Luz," and his favorite, "Tiempo III."

He was not familiar with Walt Whitman, so I gave him "Song of Myself." Sometime later I also gave him León Felipe's work on Whitman. This was the first time that Ernesto heard of this great Spaniard, whom he would later meet in Mexico. Finally, I presented him with "Contracanto a Walt Whitman," by the Santo Domingan poet Pedro Mir.

It was a pleasant surprise to discover that we shared philosophical points of view. Admiring the fortitude with which he endured his illness I was reminded of Rudyard Kipling's famous poem "If." I had learned it as a little girl and it has never ceased to be a source of strength and life for me. I recited the first few verses and he continued to the end; the poem was also an inspiration for him. Another book that we discovered had impressed both of us since our early youth was *Ariel,* the classic essay by José Enrique Rodó.

One day when we were reading, he took my hand and placed it on his forehead, holding it there while he told me how good it felt. Afterward, when we said goodbye, he kissed me, and I told myself I was accepting the gesture just to cheer him up, not because there was anything serious between us.

Ernesto had given me Curzio Malaparte's *The Skin* and *Huasipungo* by Ecuadorian writer Jorge Icaza, whom he had met in Guayaquil. The first book led us to study the Yankee penetration of Europe, especially in Italy, and the second the life of the Indians not only in Ecuador but also in Peru, Bolivia, and Guatemala. Another book he gave me was Fallas' *Mamita Yunai.* The reading of this book set us off into a discussion of the United Fruit monopoly throughout Central America.

To help him find work, I introduced him to Harold White, the North American whom I knew through Benjamín de Yurre, a Cuban from the group affiliated with Socarrás. I had been asked to translate his book on Marxism, and I thought that perhaps Ernesto could take the job instead of me. He needed the money more than I did. I offered to help him with it. He accepted and we undertook the job of translating the book together. Since I knew more English than he did and he more about Marxism than I, we had a very good basis for collaboration.

Ernesto and White became good friends, and through Ernesto I became better acquainted with White and actually grew to trust him. Once Ernesto told me: "This is a good gringo. He is tired of capitalism and wants to lead a new life."

Ernesto, White, and I became fast friends, although we continued seeing the people in Myrna's group. The three of us began going on Sunday picnics, during which it became a custom to have long discussions between Ernesto, with his crude English, and White on subjects that ranged from the international situation to Marxism, Lenin, Engels, Stalin, Freud, science in the Soviet Union, and Pavlov's conditioned reflexes.

Our friendship with White developed so well that at one point he, with his North American practicality, suggested that we should rent a house where the three of us could live, and very generously offered to pay the rent. This, he said, would be very convenient for him; he suffered from diabetes and was in need of special food. The food bill would be shared by him and me. Ernesto was also enthusiastic about the idea; this would solve his lodging problem. For my part, I didn't share their enthusiasm because it would mean taking care of a house. Trying to convince me, Ernesto again promised that he would make no advances. I told him that this had nothing to do with my lack of interest but that, since I was working and involved in political activity, I needed the remaining time to study. A situation like the one proposed would entail numerous problems for me. Fortunately, White didn't acquire the house he had been offered, which meant that I didn't have to refuse.

I REMEMBER AN outing in San Juan Sacatepéquez. After walking around the countryside we sat down to a barbecue that Ernesto had prepared. Later, when we wanted to return to the city, we discovered that a religious celebration was being held in the town and that it would be difficult to find transportation to get back. White tried to convince us to stay in a hotel. I objected meekly: "What will they think in my boardinghouse?" Ernesto looked at me and decided that he would find a way to get me back no matter what. "We will find a way, even if it's only you who is able to return," he said. Thanks to his efforts, the three of us were able to get back on a crowded bus.

This gesture on his part again heightened my opinion of him. I remember how, at the beginning of our friendship, he had once warned me against men who lie, having observed how some of my comrades were courting me. Above all, he had warned me in regard to one Peruvian who constantly flirted with me. I never took it seriously, but Ernesto had taken me aside and said, "Be careful, he is married; you know men always lie."

There was mutual affection between us. He knew me and could anticipate my reactions. One time, realizing how much I was missing my family, he said to me: "You should never have left your country." Another time, already aware of my point of view from our endless political discussions, he asked, "How can a woman who thinks like a Communist belong to APRA?" Like many student leaders, I belonged to that party because I thought it was the radical party that would bring about the revolution. My belief was based on some of APRA's literature: "Anti-Imperialism in APRA," "Letters to the Prisoners," etc. We truly believed that the APRA leaders wanted to start a revolution, to transform our unjust society. Unfortunately, every day brought me closer to the conclusion that this was not so.

5

BEFORE ERNESTO HAD that asthma attack, in speaking about his travels, he expressed his great admiration for Machu Picchu, the Peruvian ruins. We talked broadly about the Inca civilization and the present-day misery of the Indian. He surprised me with his knowledge and sensitivity. He knew about the exploited state in which our Indians lived, and he understood the psychological barriers between the Indians and *mestizos* and the whites, who had been exploiting them for many centuries. He then told me that he had written an article on Machu Picchu for a Panamanian magazine, and the next day he brought it me for me to read. It was a good article, illustrated with photographs, three of which he had personally taken under the direction of a professional photographer he met on his second visit to the ruins. After Ernesto had gone, a coworker came to my office with Venezuelan exile Guillermo Salazar Meneses. Salazar saw the article Ernesto had left on my desk and became very enthusiastic. He told me that he would have it published in a Guatemalan periodical. Unfortunately, Ernesto didn't accept the offer because he considered the article to be very superficial. Later he scolded me, telling me heatedly, "I gave the article to you to read, not to show around." I explained that it had been an accident, and that there had been no intention of anything on my part. The incident made me think. I wondered whether he might have given me the article as an homage to my country.

When Ernesto recovered, he wanted to go to the little town of San José de Pinula, where the City of Children was located. This city, a project begun by Juan José Orozco Posadas, was situated among pines and other marvelous greenery. It was a camp for boys and girls with discipline problems, children who had run away from home or were caught in petty thievery or other misdemeanors; that is, children who were in the first stages of delinquency. Orozco Posadas was a teacher with exciting ideas; he was sincerely preoccupied with children and young people, applying himself to reforming those who had taken the wrong road through no fault of their own but because of the poor structure of society. He was more influenced by the example of a North American priest than by the children's welfare efforts that were being carried out in the Soviet Union, but in any case it was a worthwhile effort. The work being done there caught the attention of the Peruvian exiles, and we got together for a day and participated in the construction of the city. I told Ernesto about it, and he became interested and asked me to take him. We went there alone, the two of us. We didn't work this time; we simply strolled around talking to the boys and girls. Later we attended a talk given by Orozco Posadas to the students. Our impression after our visit was that this City of Children was attaining its objectives. The children were being reeducated in a liberal and communal atmosphere where they were encouraged to accept responsibility for themselves. The visit opened up a new topic of conversation on the conditions of our continent's children. Victims of hunger, disease, illiteracy, and overall abandonment, these children grow into adulthood easy prey for crime and constitute a vital human loss in our development. All this is a result of the defective social structure, of exploitative ruling oligarchies, and of the penetration of Yankee capitalists who swallow up our riches. Obviously we agreed that this would be one of the first concerns of a revolution. In passing, we commented on what was being done in the Soviet Union for the benefit of children and how no effort was spared to care for children whose mothers were at work.

Going out into the countryside on Sundays became a habit. I liked it very much because it was a change from the routine of everyday city life, and I especially enjoyed the quiet of the rural atmosphere. It also was the best way to get to know the different little towns surrounding the Guatemalan capital. During these outings Ernesto was fond of recalling times spent in the Argentine city of Córdoba and he told me many stories from those days: about his friends, school parties, sports, horse races, etc. He loved to make a barbecue à la Argentina, and so most of the time we would buy a piece of meat and some fruit and he would improvise a roasting pit with a few branches and cook our lunch.

Our perspectives on life and our role in society were in complete agreement: We didn't believe that our objective as professionals was to earn money, to make our personal fortunes. We were aware that we had received from society the benefits of knowledge and culture, and that whatever we had learned and would learn in the future had to serve society. We couldn't be happy amid exploitation and misery, and therefore we were determined to dedicate our lives and efforts to remedying these social evils, no matter the risks.

The fact is that I had been thinking that way for a long time; I had taken a definite political position, and that was why I was in exile. But it was during this time that Ernesto began to define his attitude toward these questions. In theory he was already a partisan, but it was not until Guatemala that he adopted the role. It was there that he came to know other exiles and to learn about men who either had died or been taken prisoner as a result of real struggles.

Engels's *Anti-Dühring*, which we had both read, became the subject of many conversations. From this book, we learned about life philosophy and the socialist conception of the individual as part of society. We were also in agreement that we both had to improve ourselves individually, to contribute better to society's goals. I can say unequivocally that we shared a sense of the "agony of life," that is, we weren't afraid of death. We saw death as something natural that we could accept on behalf of society. It was somewhat the concept of Unamuno, with whom we were also familiar at the time.

We disagreed about Sartre and Freud. Ernesto was a follower of their teachings. But while I recognized the monumental character of their works and the great contributions they had made to art and psychology, I could only partially accept their points of view. Sartre's works were fashionable in Argentina, and Ernesto, an avid Sartre admirer, was an expert on existentialism. As a political militant, I had already rejected strictly individualistic problems and had adopted a role of struggle. Of course, I consider Sartre's and the existentialists' denunciation of the system and of society to be valid. But it's not enough to detect and expose the ills of capitalistic society. One must do something to change this society to its very roots, and this requires a different approach: concrete work toward that goal. Nor could I accept a so-called defeatist philosophy, a nihilistic analysis in which the only thing left is suicide. One *must* find a way.

In my opinion the problems denounced by Sartre weren't universal but specific, having to do more with the developed societies of Europe. Perhaps Argentina, particularly Buenos Aires, could fit into this category. But for the majority of our semideveloped Latin American societies with a fully formed capitalist crust, the problems weren't the same. In our countries the struggle was more demanding, a little more primitive. It was a struggle to reach true social justice, a fight against exploitation, hunger, ill health, illiteracy, and the dismal levels of life in our villages. These were the immediate tasks that must absorb our energies.

In any case, Ernesto was a great believer in Sartre, although as our discussions continued, he became less of an existentialist. Nor was I against the charges Sartre made, with the help of psychology, but I still believed that the individual's problems weren't the only ones, that the fundamental difficulties arose from the societal structure. On this point Ernesto agreed.

Perhaps he admired Sartre so much because he had read him more than I, who knew his first book, *Existentialism,* later *The Age of Reason,* and had seen the play *The Respectful Prostitute.* Ernesto, knew all of those and gave his views as well on *The Wall, Being and Nothingness, Nausea,* and *Dirty Hands.*

"Of course it's true," he once said to me, commenting on the last work, "that Sartre has attacked the Communist Party."

I responded that what Sartre was attacking was the deformations of Communism and Marxism, an attitude I agreed with. I praised Sartre for coming forward with such denunciations, thus becoming for me practically a militant, though not a Communist— a man with a sense of responsibility for society, and as such worthy of my sympathy and respect.

We saw *The Respectful Prostitute* together, and we discussed not only the racial problems but all the individual problems Sartre presents in that work. The mise-en-scène was pretty bad, but the presentation was faithful to the text.

Ernesto was also passionate about Freud and his interpretation of life based on sexual drives. I didn't wholly share that concept; to me it was incomplete. How could one explain the existence of individuals like the political fighters—normal, complete beings whose motivations certainly did not stem from sexual issues? There were many such examples in history, and we knew of a number of cases closer to us; for example, among the Latin American exiles living in Guatemala. Instead, I believed that man, in accordance with the Marxist interpretation, is a product of his environment, of his needs, and of his contradictions with that environment. Of course, there could be a sexual motivation during the first years, but when these problems are all solved in a positive manner, men are normal human beings who could freely accept their responsibility to society.

We had read a little of Adler and Jung, Ernesto much more than I. We discussed them at length on numerous occasions. The talks seemed to be interminable, but we were always aware that the point was to acquire a greater knowledge in order to try to understand and improve mankind. I used to quote to him from the works of two Soviet scientists on the topic of environmental influence—Michurin on nature and Pavlov on psychiatry—whereupon Ernesto began to study these works with determination. In all of our discussions, our more knowledgeable friend Harold White helped. I began to see Ernesto developing his ideas little by little toward the Marxist ideology, which he had already accepted in principle.

One day I began to see Ernesto differently. It was when he rejected an opportunity for work that had been offered to him on the condition that he join the PGT (Guatemalan Party of Labor), the Communist Party of Guatemala. The offer had come down through Herbert Zeissig, a member of the youth organization of the PGT who worked at the Institute as an agricultural technician. He worked at the same location as Myrna and me, and in addition to this we were personal friends. I had talked with Zeissig about Guevara, saying that he was an Argentine doctor who wanted to go to Petén for a year to work but that he had been asked to get his diploma revalidated, and that this was impossible because he wanted to stay in Guatemala only one more year. Since Zeissig offered to help him, I introduced them, and he in turn took Ernesto to meet the people in the Department of Statistics. Ernesto left his curriculum vitae, and they said they would let him know. One morning Zeissig[1] came to my office with the news: yes, Guevara had been accepted, but he would have to join the PGT.

---

1.   Years later Zeissig went over to the counterrevolutionary ranks. We never knew whether his attitude on the above occasion was personal or that of the PGT.

All this sounded very strange and I was curious to find out Ernesto's reaction. I asked him to come to the office and told him the news.

"You tell him," he snapped angrily, "that when I want to join the party I will do so on my own initiative, not out of any ulterior motive!"

I admired his reaction. He needed a job to survive, yet he was incapable of doing anything contrary to his moral and revolutionary principles. I suggested we call Zeissig so that Ernesto could tell him himself, which he did. I said nothing as they talked.

A few days later, when he calmed down a bit, he explained further: "It's not that I disagree with the Communist ideology, it's the method I don't like. They shouldn't get members this way. It's all false."

6

ERNESTO WAS ALWAYS welcome in the home of Señora de Toriello, as well as by her niece María, who at times was in charge of the house. The other guests—two middle-aged Guatemalan ladies and a pharmaceutical salesman from El Salvador—also liked him.

I remember one evening—it was in mid-March 1954—Ernesto seemed serious when he called on me, and more serious when he discovered there was a small birthday party in progress. I was dancing; he was over at the side of the room and he seemed to want to talk to me. When we finally made our way to each other, he said sarcastically, "I didn't realize you were so frivolous . . . you really like to dance!"

It wasn't frivolity, I explained to him: I simply enjoyed dancing from time to time. Besides, dancing was a way to forget worries and sadness for a while.

Then he handed me a handwritten poem. It was a formal proposal of marriage.

It impressed me profoundly, but I couldn't show great enthusiasm, as he was also telling me that he had had an affair with a nurse in the hospital where he helped out. So I told him if he preferred the nurse he should go away with her: I wasn't interested in anything conditional. Then he laughed and said he had told me about the nurse only to see my reaction; he had already decided that the affair was of no importance; it was over. He asked me to be his girlfriend; later on, we might get married. If it were up to him, we would get married immediately.

I told him that I also loved him, but not enough to marry him just yet and that I thought the most important issue at the time was the political struggle. The decision of marriage was a very difficult one for me; first I had to accomplish something for society, and to do that I had to be free. He answered that those were Aprista prejudices, and that it was wrong to think that political activists shouldn't marry, when in effect it was a path to greater fulfillment. He referred to Marx and Lenin, saying that marriage had not impeded them in their struggle. On the contrary, their wives supported them.

I could see the reasoning in his argument, but I was still unsure and doubted very much that I would ever be convinced. I knew that he had much to contribute to society. We had talked about what marriage meant to us on several occasions; personally, I didn't feel that women reached fulfillment and self-realization through marriage. In my view, a woman should be contributing to social progress and therefore had to prepare for it and become financially independent. When the time came to select a partner, she would do so freely and not because she needed a provider. If they got married and didn't get along, or the partner fell in love with another, then they would discuss it openly and make the necessary decision, even if it entailed a separation. Our opinions on the matter coincided.

The poem was short but beautiful and forceful. Through it he told me that he did not desire beauty alone but, more than that, a comrade. I kept it as it was precious to me, a beautiful memento of him, together with another poem he wrote for our daughter, Hildita, the day he left for Cuba aboard the ship *Granma*. In January 1957 my purse, along with the poems in it, was stolen in the streets of Lima, and, in spite of the ads promising a reward for its return, I never got it back.

Toward the end of March 1954, in addition to the translation job, Ernesto had joined Ñico and the other Cubans in selling various articles in the provinces. Obviously this brought in very little money, but it was something and it helped. In April, Ernesto moved into the boardinghouse that the government set up to house the Cuban exiles, but by the middle of the month Ñico and several other Cubans left for Mexico City. The only Cubans remaining in the house were Mario Dalmau and Cheche, who were not close friends like the others.

Since Ernesto was left without anyone to help him directly, I spoke with Elena de Holst and she offered her house. She loved Ernesto like a son because she had one the same age. He was very grateful but didn't accept. He wanted no favors. He took his sleeping bag and started spending his nights on the country club grounds. Early in the morning he would arrive at Señora de Toriello's, where I lived, to ask us for hot water for his maté. We always kept fresh fruit for him; he never accepted anything else. In the evenings he would return and eat only fruit or salad; to avoid the asthma attacks, he still kept very strictly to his diet.

For some time now he had been awaiting an answer from the Ministry of Education, where he had sought employment as an intern in a teacher-training center. Toward the end of April he was granted the position.

MYRNA WAS VERY active in the leadership of the Democratic Youth; she was forever organizing meetings and social outings. One Saturday evening she arranged a trip to Amatitlán with the Cubans, some Peruvians, Ernesto, myself, and her group from the youth organization. We recited poems by some young Guatemalan poets, among whom were Raúl Leiva and Otto Raúl Gonzales, and sang revolutionary songs, some Guatemalan, some Spanish. Ernesto was very happy, especially during the poetry recitations. We built fires and roasted sausages and ate them with tortillas.

When he accepted the invitation, Ernesto had told me that he would remain there alone for the rest of the weekend. I hadn't believed him, but when he arrived at the departure point he had a knapsack containing his sleeping bag, thermos, and things to prepare his maté. Under his arm was a packet of books: the *Popol Vuh*, *Annals of the Cachiqueles*, Franz Blom's *Life of the Mayans*, and Silvanus Morley's *The Ancient Maya*. We arrived at 8 p.m. that night, and at midnight, when we were preparing to return, Ernesto stayed, despite Myrna's and the others' advice that he should return with the group. Quietly but firmly he stated that he wanted to be alone. I stopped insisting; I was beginning to understand that he liked the lonely beauty of the Guatemalan countryside. Perhaps it reminded him of his trips in Córdoba.

He called my office as soon as he returned on Monday morning, and came to visit that evening. He told me that he had had a very good time and had enjoyed reading about Mayan culture. For food he had bought fruit and meat, and he felt fine. He commented on the books he had read, which roused my curiosity about Blom and Morley. I understood that he loved the country, losing himself in books, and being alone. I liked those things too.

THE YOUTH GROUP was celebrating the founding of their Democratic Alliance with a sports jamboree. The fiesta was to take place somewhere in the surrounding countryside. Ernesto, White, Myrna and her group, and I went to the Alameda de Chimaltenango, where there was a sports field and swimming pool. Some people went strolling; others organized games or went swimming. We decided to walk in the fields with White and a Honduran woman accompanied by her young daughter. Ernesto was carrying his ubiquitous maté things, and from time to time we drank maté Argentine style, sucking the bitter tea through a straw.

I remember we saw Communist congressman Carlos Manuel Pellecer doing calisthenics. He didn't even say hello. It seemed to us he felt self-important with his deputy's post and had to show off. Ernesto commented to me: "There's a typical representative of the ruling bureaucracy." We were very surprised that he was a representative of the PGT, a man like Pellecer, who had been removed from a diplomatic post in London for misusing embassy funds—an incident that was public knowledge. Ernesto later met him when he took asylum in the Argentine embassy.

After the triumph of the Cuban Revolution, Pellecer came to Havana looking for work. Due to the position he held within the PGT, he was allowed to enter the country as an editor of the daily newspaper *Hoy,* and he moved about in public-administration circles. Taking advantage of the fact that he had met Ernesto in Guatemala, he was granted an interview. I met him later in Cuba through mutual friends, and although he greeted me with great courtesy, I couldn't help saying, with a bit of irony, "Now things are different, not at all like when you were so proud of being a congressman." And I went on to tell him of the impression that I had the day we saw him doing calisthenics.

We didn't understand it at the time, but perhaps when Pellecer arrived in Cuba he had already been recruited as an agent of imperialism. He repaid the privilege of his position as newspaper editor as well as the channels that the revolutionary government opened for him with betrayal, manifested by his nauseating book, in which he contorts a few facts into a wildly imaginative structure.

Ernesto decided he would go to El Salvador for a few days while he waited for an answer on the job he had applied for. He had a few pesos left from his translations, although this money was barely enough to get around. He was bound for Puerto Barrios and then to the capital city, San Salvador.

When he came to say goodbye, he left his suitcase with me, along with the original manuscript of his research on Latin American doctors and the diary in which he succinctly recorded his travels. I thought I wouldn't see him again, but he assured me that he would write to me.

"Let me know where you'll be so that I can send you your things," I said.

He laughed and answered, "I'll be back, don't you believe me?"

He left me thinking that even if he didn't come back it was good to have known him and helped him. He would do something for society.

He returned a week later and showed up in my office with no warning. He laughed teasingly at my surprise and said: "Aha! I startled you. I bet you thought I wouldn't come back." He told me that he had only just arrived; dirty and tired, he decided to go over to Elena's house to take a shower and change. He was just passing by my office and came up to say hello. He was on his way to the teachers' center to find out about his job application. He told me that he would come to pick me up at six that evening and left. Indeed, it had been a surprise: I had thought he wouldn't be back.

When we met outside my office, he told me the good news: he had been accepted and would start the next day. Later he talked about his trip. He had gone to Puerto Barrios by train and had worked there for two and a half days carrying banana sacks. The working conditions were terrible, the sacks so heavy they wore away the skin on his body. I didn't believe the story at the beginning, so he showed me his calluses. He had left the place, he said, without bothering to collect his earnings, having achieved what he set out to do when he took the job: find out what the work was like. Again by train he went on to San Salvador. He was there four days, enough to see the great oppression under which the people lived. He told me stories about the large *fincas* (estates), with their private guards who would arrest and at times shoot peasants who protested or laid claim to their land. He spoke of the meetings he had had with several groups of workers and of how he had tried to encourage them to continue their struggle against the system. The police had followed and questioned him. He was almost arrested and was forced to leave the country in haste. His account led us to talk about the terrible massacre of 1932, when the forces of General Maximiliano Hernández Martínez killed some thirty-two thousand workers.

TOWARD THE END of April, Harold White came to see me. "Hilda," he said, "it seems there's going to be an attack on Guatemala with the support of the U.S.A. Aren't you leaving? You might be arrested . . ." I told him I wasn't going.

Since Ernesto held the position as intern in the teachers' center, he slept there now, and he had to report for work at nine o'clock in the morning. So he began coming to visit me every afternoon after work. We would then attend a political meeting, stroll together, or simply sit at my house talking. But that routine was changed by the bombing that started in early May. It was done by one or two pirate planes in each raid, day or night, with the aim of starting a psychological war. At first they bombed only military installations; later they began bombing slum areas, and finally the presidential palace.

Ernesto joined the comrades of the Youth Alliance in their night guard duty. A total blackout had been ordered, and they were in charge of seeing that it was respected. I in turn had signed a public pronouncement, issued by the exiles, in support of the Guatemalan Revolution. At the office I had already organized a woman's brigade to take food to the workers on night guard duty.

Facing the imminent invasion, all the political parties joined together to form an emergency committee that would serve as counsel to President Jacobo Arbenz Guzmán. It was known that an army was being trained in Honduras to invade Guatemala. On June 25 the president spoke on national radio urging everyone to unite and resist, ending with a promise to the effect of: "We shall not retreat one inch, not this twenty-fifth of June nor any other day."

In addition to the bombing, rumors helped sustain a kind of psychological warfare: The word went around that when the "liberators" came, they were going to execute all the revolutionaries and their families.

Ernesto told me how he constantly urged the Youth Alliance to go to the front to fight, and that many youngsters, encouraged by him, were willing. He said that time and again the suggestion was presented to the PGT, but the only answer they got was that the army was already taking care of everything and that the people should not worry. I know that Guevara and other Latin American revolutionaries formulated plans to improve defenses and withstand the small invading force of some seven hundred men, mainly mercenaries. But no one could counsel the president directly. He saw no one and listened only to the secretary-general of the PGT, José Manuel Fortuny. This was no secret; every revolutionary knew it at the time and talked about it after the disaster.

This whole situation was undermining the revolutionary leaders' faith in victory. I remember very well a woman leader who came to my office and said: "Hilda, aren't you going to seek asylum? We have been thinking of advising you to do so."

I was very surprised. This was early in June, and the people I expected to be the firmest in their convictions were already talking about asylum. I thanked her for her kind advice and kept my thoughts to myself. But I asked Ernesto to come to my office. During those days he was reading and writing about agrarian reform, doing research for an economist. He came immediately, and I told him what the woman had said.

"It's happening, Ernesto. Think about what she said to me . . . if those who should be leading the defense are thinking that way, what will the people think?"

I was being partially unjust at the time. Afterward, when various officers were shown to be traitors and Arbenz resigned, I found out that many workers and peasants, and some of the political leaders, took up arms and defended the regime.

Ernesto agreed with me that the attack was imminent, that it was very difficult to predict what would happen, and that the woman leader's warning was a bad sign. But it didn't prove anything: certainly the government would be defended with the help of the people in spite of the cowardice of some of the leaders. We reaffirmed our decision to help the Guatemalan people although we were aware that we were risking our lives.

On three different occasions friends advised me to flee the country or to seek asylum. Perhaps I would have done so if Ernesto hadn't been there. But his firm, enthusiastic attitude encouraged me. And, in truth, I also wanted to help the Guatemalan people defend their revolution against this right-wing, Yankee-financed attack.

On June 18 the mercenaries, commanded by Castillo Armas, crossed the border into Guatemalan territory, with air support, and took some small towns. At the beginning there was some resistance; later, according to what we heard, there was none. Every day we would discuss the news and commentaries.

One of my windows was broken by machine-gun bullets during one of the bombings of the presidential palace. The owner of the house had me move to an inner room that looked over a patio and was next to the kitchen. This was a fateful incident because of the cook. She was an Indian woman from Quezaltenango, and incidentally a very good cook, who was extremely Catholic and who defended the Yankee invasion. Afterward we learned that she was a member of the clandestine antigovernment movement and played a more important role in our lives than we had imagined: We believed that it was she who denounced us as revolutionaries.

Daily discussions around the dinner table were routine in my house. It was during one such evening that the cook declared that she was in favor of the invasion. This surprised both Ernesto and me; she understood nothing of what the revolution meant for the people. This incident became a new topic of discussion for Ernesto and me: the necessity of acquainting the people with the goals of a revolution, as well as with the distorting influence of the institutional church.

Our outlooks coincided in so many areas. I used to tell Ernesto that I belonged to the Aprista Party only because it was a means, an instrument by which to take power and build a new society; that the problem was to make a revolution with the people and to do so it was necessary to take away the special privileges of the ruling oligarchy, a class that had been in power for centuries, and nationalize our natural resources that were unjustly in the hands of foreign landholders. As for the Latin American problem, it was a fact that our countries had fought together since the struggle for independence, and only this close collaboration made success possible. Both San Martín and Bolívar had to liberate other nations to consolidate the independence of their own countries: Bolívar above all represented the ideal of the common struggle necessary to face the enormous power of the United States; Martín was also a clear example. Change couldn't be brought about by a coup d'état, through collusion with the military, or merely by removing a military leader. If this were so, I would be willing to risk my life to have Odría disappear. But this would be no solution: another thick-skulled military man would be put at the head of the government and nothing would be gained.

In general Ernesto agreed with me, but he didn't believe that APRA was a revolutionary party. He said that Haya de la Torre had gone against his first anti-imperialist platform of 1928, that he no longer spoke of fighting the Yankees or for the nationalization of the Panama Canal, and that if he ever took power he would not carry out the People's Revolution. I answered that many of us, the young leaders of the Aprista Party, believed that this abandonment of the main objectives of the struggle were tactical moves, and that once in power APRA would carry out a true transformation.

"Yes, but how will it reach power?" he said. "Through elections? That will never happen. And if it compromises with the right and gets the support of the U.S.A.—which is the way it's usually done in our countries—that won't constitute a revolution." He continued: "In that, Perón has done something; he has protected the workers; he has done something to take away economic power from the oligarchy and, to some extent, from the imperialists. But he had much more to accomplish; he had to fight against the landowners so that the revolution could go deep."

Our conversations would then drift into the subject of what a coup d'état meant. We had both read Curzio Malaparte's *Technique of Coup d'État* and other books on the subject. We agreed that if the coup d'état meant, as it did in 1917, the taking of power through a mass struggle with a good vanguard leadership, this could be the beginning of a revolution. But he doubted whether this experience could be repeated in Latin America because the situation was different. Here, in this part of the continent, Yankee imperialism was a decisive factor we would need to confront head-on if a revolution were the aim.

As for the Communist parties, Ernesto respected them and considered their theoretical approach correct. At the same time he sensed that they weren't working for solidarity with the people; they were drifting away from the working masses instead of toward them. For me, the true nature of the Communist parties was much clearer. I used to explain my disapproval to him for how they confused the masses and often entered into alliances with the right to reach a position of power, thus obscuring the goals. But I did believe that it was necessary to build a new society where human relations could be different, where profit wouldn't be the only motivating force. And I did admire the Soviet Revolution and all it meant for that country and humanity, and for the making of a new man in a new society. I particularly admired the achievement of equal rights for women.

"Why are you an Aprista," he asked, "when you think like a Communist? I think you have a psychological problem from your childhood; you have a Joan of Arc complex in wanting to sacrifice yourself for the fatherland." I answered that it wasn't a complex and went on to explain that I would never act like that, because it wouldn't be useful. All of this confirmed for me the fact that his thinking about the struggles of our peoples was sincere, and not motivated by some sense of failure connected with his illness. Ernesto wouldn't fight merely to be sacrificed but because he was convinced of the reasons for the struggle. On the other hand, his arguments revealed that he was still influenced by Freud, and I differed with him on that.

Another area in which we had completely different opinions was that of the Catholics. At the time, he thought that nothing could be done with the Catholics and that they were holding back the revolution. I agreed with respect to the institution itself—that is, the ecclesiastical authorities were allied with the oligarchies to maintain a structure that gave them certain privileges—but I felt that the Catholic masses were different. Besides, it was a problem that we had to take into account since the majorities in our countries are Catholic and there were large numbers of Catholics who were Christians of good faith. No true Christian could oppose a society in which there is no exploitation since Christ himself preached against injustice and the rich; for me Christ was a social activist later mythologized by the Church. But large parts of our illiterate masses who allowed priests to guide them weren't really Catholic: they participated in the mass ritual as a substitution for ancient cults that were based mostly on natural forces.

Ernesto agreed with this, and added that in the most developed countries of our continent, such as his, a large part of the population was Catholic, but their Catholicism was merely a social convenience and not a vital belief practiced in daily life. Every day, those countries were further de-Catholicized because the Church did not follow its own precepts. But we were never able to come to a full agreement. I was confident that within the Catholic Church a revolution would take place and that part of the church would join the true proletarian revolution. Ernesto didn't think this would happen; he said that the institution would prevail and that it was impossible to count on militant Catholics to make a revolution, but that it was possible to count on those Catholics who abandoned the faith in the name of reason.

7

DESPITE THE FACT that we were busy with the defense of the revolution, we didn't stop observing and analyzing what was happening daily. The people weren't being given arms, and—except in Puerto Barrios, where a woman leader, Haydée Godoy, organized a few workers on her own and repelled another small invasion—there was no effort to try to enlist the support of the people. All hope was placed on the shoulders of the regular army. We could foresee the fall of the government and this was cause for great pain, especially for Ernesto; he was convinced that if the people were armed the attack could be successfully repelled.

So he wrote an article. He dictated it to me over three or four afternoons, and he called it "I Saw the Fall of Jacobo Arbenz." The article ran about ten or twelve pages. Unfortunately I made only one copy, and he kept the original. The special circumstances that later befell us explain the disappearance of both copies. My copy was more than likely burned by the Guatemalan police who confiscated all of my belongings, which of course included all my writings and political literature, when they searched my room before taking me to jail. As for the original copy, Ernesto kept it with him. Later, when he could find no further hiding place, and the police were closing in, he was offered asylum in the Argentine embassy by Nicasio Sánchez Toranzo, the acting ambassador. There a few comrades had the opportunity to read this short essay. Among them was Mario Dalmau, a participant in the Moncada attack, who later referred to the article in the special *Granma* newspaper edition honoring Che Guevara.

This was Ernesto's first political article. In it he blamed Yankee imperialism for the fall of the Arbenz government, and he emphasized the need to struggle against it and the oligarchy that supported it. The article marked a new stage in Ernesto's development: He had acquired a concrete awareness of the problems in our Latin American countries, for the most part governed with the approval and intervention of the United States. For the first time, he articulated his decision to fight openly against imperialism wherever it was. Up to that point, he used to say, he was merely a sniper, criticizing the political panorama of our America from a theoretical point of view. From here on he was convinced that the struggle against the oligarchic system and Yankee imperialism must be an armed one, supported by the people. He was absolutely certain that if Arbenz had armed the people, his government wouldn't have fallen.

I will try to reconstruct the basic points of the article: First, he analyzed the world situation and the struggle between the two camps, capitalist and socialist. He said that the socialist camp, begun by the Soviet Revolution of 1917, continued through the Chinese Revolution, and later the recently initiated Algerian Revolution; that it would widen because there were many countries in Latin America, Asia, and Africa governed by exploitative systems that depended, directly or indirectly, on imperialism. Revolution was therefore a world phenomenon in which Latin America was called upon to play an important part.

Ernesto placed Guatemala among the most exploited countries of Latin America and argued that, like the remainder of the continent, it was penetrated by the interests of Yankee monopolies that deformed its economy. Corrupting its ruling class, these foreign interests placed and replaced governments at will, turning the national bourgeoisie into easily manipulated puppets.

These bourgeoisies made no attempt to defend their nations' sovereignty, but under these pressures turned against even democratic nationalist governments, as was the case in Guatemala. The Latin American bourgeoisies, as in all exploited countries, couldn't be counted on to carry out a true transformation of a politico-economic system. The basic question was that of direct struggle against Yankee imperialism that supported these ruling classes. Third, positions such as those taken by Haya de la Torre, Betancourt, Figueres, and the like, constituted a betrayal of the true revolution and independence of our countries. Ernesto pointed out very clearly that the fall of the Guatemalan government was due to a clash with Yankee monopoly interests, specifically those of the United Fruit Company, whose interests were hurt by the agrarian reform; the Electric Bond and Share Company, which monopolized the power industry; and AT&T, which, in Guatemala as in many of our other countries, owns all the telephones. These corporations encouraged the reactionary forces of Guatemala and financed the invasion; furthermore, they recruited mercenary elements, trained them, and aided them in all aspects. (Years later, in 1961, we would witness the invasion of the Bay of Pigs, financed and supported by the Yankees, in which the Cuban people, led by Fidel Castro, defeated the imperialists for the first time in this part of the world.)

The article stated that the struggle in Guatemala had to lead to the nationalization of our resources and to the socialization of the means of production. The second stage of the Guatemalan Revolution, therefore, must have their reclamations as its objective and that this was only a part of continental and world revolution.

By witnessing the attack of Yankee imperialism on democracy in Guatemala, Ernesto committed himself as an anti-imperialist fighter and decided to take active part in the struggle no matter which country he might be in. The final sentence in the article was: "The struggle begins now."

One day while he was dictating the article to me, two planes were bombing several locations in the capital. We were listening to the roar of the motors when Ernesto said, "Let's hope these SOBs don't blow up the whole house," referring to the fact that they had already damaged the window of the first room I had. He had raised his voice in his excitement, and I told him to lower it. I didn't trust the cook.

Ernesto continued his activities. In the mornings he'd go to the teachers' center; in the afternoons he wrote for a while and then read about agrarian reform for the research project on which he was collaborating. In the early evenings we would go for walks and talk. At night he went to the Youth Alliance for his night duty against blackout violations. He suffered moments of great desperation when, in spite of his eagerness, he realized that he wouldn't be allowed to fight. A group of young people shared his desire to fight, but the authorization had to come from the military command, and it never came.

During the last week before Arbenz's resignation there were daylight bombings aimed at creating an atmosphere of fear in the population. I witnessed several fainting spells and nervous breakdowns among the secretaries in my office. All of the personnel were generally very tense and uneasy; there was hardly any talking. Like me, Ernesto noted any aura of insecurity because it was a sign of a lack of political awareness and loss of trust in the leadership. Again he stated that if the people were told the truth about the need to fight the superior forces of the North American imperialists, and if they were given arms, the revolution could still be saved. "Furthermore," he pointed out, "even if the capital were to fall, the fight could continue in the interior of the country, in Guatemala's mountainous areas."

Two days before the fall of the government a coworker came in early and said the government was falling. There were tears in his eyes. His brother was a colonel at command headquarters. The minister of defense had called them in to inform them that Ambassador Puerifoy was demanding the resignation of Arbenz or else a full-on imperialist attack would be launched; there was a North American aircraft carrier off the coast. Thus pressured, the general staff demanded that Arbenz resign. Arbenz gave in and promised his capitulation within the next twenty-four hours.

Ernesto was not at all surprised. He had been expecting it because of the Yankee pressure. But he still insisted: "I believe if Arbenz repudiates his general staff and goes after the support of the people, giving them arms, he can go up to the mountains and fight no matter how many years it lasts."

He sought out political leaders who were his friends and true revolutionaries at that time—among them were Marco Antonio Villamar and Alfonso Bauer Paiz—to communicate his idea to them. Villamar told him that he had gone with a large group of workers to the arsenal to ask for weapons and that the military had refused, ordering them to get out quickly if they didn't want to be shot. Bauer Paiz told Ernesto that he already knew about Arbenz's resignation and that he was very upset because the president hadn't consulted the emergency committee, of which Bauer himself was a member.

Nothing remained to be done but await reprisals. My friend, the woman leader, visited me again to tell me that she and her family were going to seek asylum like all the political leaders, and that Arbenz and Fortuny had already left. They were the first. The president, having recorded his resignation speech, sent it to Radio Guatemala and went to the Mexican embassy, where he asked for and received asylum. I thanked her for the information and told her that I would leave the country but that I wouldn't take asylum. That afternoon, as Ernesto and I sat talking, the news of the president's resignation, of his and Fortuny's asylum in the Mexican embassy, was all over town. This was particularly painful for us because we were convinced that the last and true effort hadn't been made, and popular support hadn't been sought—the people hadn't been armed to expel the invaders, or at least to fight. That afternoon, June 26, the national radio station of Guatemala broadcast the resignation of President Arbenz, causing great consternation among the people in favor of the revolution. Almost all the political leaders and their families had taken asylum in one or another of the already-crowded Latin American embassies.

What to do? Ernesto said that he would go to Mexico and work there for a while; afterward he hoped to go to China. He tried to convince me to go with him and marry him in Mexico, but I explained that I wanted to return to Peru, and if that wasn't possible, to go south to Argentina. I asked him for his family's address so that they could help me establish connections there. I didn't have a passport and my only document was a safe-conduct as an exile, so I had to begin the process of getting a passport or a reentry permit from my embassy. Thus we parted. Ernesto insisted, laughing, that we would one day meet again in Mexico and marry. I, of course, didn't believe him.

In the meantime, it was of absolute necessity that we move from our respective houses and prepare for our imminent departure with the utmost discretion. I had some very close friends, the Mendoza sisters, who were elderly, single, and devout Catholics. They liked me very much. It turned out that the chief of police, Colonel Mendoza, was their nephew. One of them, Graciela, called to tell me that as a political exile I was in danger of being arrested and that, because she thought so much of me, she wanted to protect me and offer me her home. I told her that I was awaiting confirmation of my application for a passport and that I hoped to be able to return to my country and my family. I thanked her for her kind gesture, which meant so much at the time. I have always thought of her as representative of Catholics of true Christian conviction, willing to sacrifice all for the principles of Christ.

I took some clothing with me, leaving the rest of my things at Señora de Toriello's, and moved to the Mendoza sisters' house. Ernesto went to live in the boardinghouse that belonged to Elena de Holst's aunt; I alone knew his address. I had stopped reporting to work because a law had been passed firing all revolutionaries from their jobs. In any case, I couldn't have continued working with such a reactionary government. Ernesto came to visit me in the afternoons for an hour or two. I remember that we read Einstein in English, and I helped him translate Pavlov from the French.

A week went by, and one afternoon I decided to bring the rest of my clothes and books from the Toriello house. After our afternoon reading I asked Ernesto to accompany me. Fortunately he declined, feeling that he shouldn't delay writing his parents to assure them that he was all right and to tell them his plans. His decision saved him.

When I arrived at the Toriello house I saw a car at the door. I was going to go on by, as I suspected something, but some plainclothes policemen stopped me. They asked me who I was and I had to tell them because Señora de Toriello's niece María, the cook, the guests, and other people in the house were present. I thought briefly of giving them false information, but I was afraid of being found out, which would make things worse. When I entered the house I saw all my books and belongings scattered about. The police began to question me immediately and their first question was whether I knew where Ernesto Guevara was. I told them that I didn't, but added that they could ask at the Argentine embassy. They wanted his description; they showed me photographs they had found among my things and wanted me to point him out, but I said that he wasn't in any of the pictures. After a while they took me and María to the Santa Teresa Women's Prison. María was allowed to leave after a few hours when she was able to prove that she and the cook had been active in Catholic organizations operating clandestinely during the period of the revolutionary governments.

I was placed in the same cell with common criminals. We slept in a large hall with the light on all night. Most of the women were in jail for robbery or homicide. We were awakened at 5 a.m. to clean the jail, and at 6 a.m. we began working. The first day I was sent to load firewood with a woman, about fifty years old, who resembled an orangutan; she had murdered her husband. She carried an axe in one hand. I walked fearfully behind her, thinking all the time she might turn around and use the axe on me. It turned out that my fears were unfounded; in fact she treated me with great consideration. The food was very bad and was handed out in banged-up tin plates; we were given bean soup prepared with raw, unseasoned beans; a few tortillas; and a spoon.

I couldn't eat the prison food; it was terrible. I drank tea and ate some apples the Mendoza sisters had sent. I spent one day loading firewood, and then I was assigned to making tortillas. The tortillas that we made were both for the jail and to be sold in the city; the prisoners, of course, did not get paid for the work.

To occupy my time constructively, I began to teach the other prisoners how to read and write. All of them, I discovered, were illiterate. At that time I was the only female political prisoner, and I protested the treatment I received to the matron, stating that I was a political exile and had the right to be treated as such. I asked her to inform the authorities of my status and request that they tell me what the charges were against me and appoint a lawyer to defend me. The matron listened without promising anything.

I received no news from outside. Once I was visited in jail by a commission from the International Red Cross. Among the group was Mr. Paiz, proprietor of the cafeteria across from my office, who knew me. He promised to help me to make my position as a political exile known to the government.

This visit took place on the fourth day of my imprisonment. I had already notified the warden that if I were not set free within the next twenty-four hours I would go on a hunger strike. She in turn informed the commission and asked them to try to dissuade me. They tried but I refused. The warden added: "She has not had anything but tea for four days."

The day that I was supposed to start my hunger strike two Peruvians came to visit me, Nicanor Mujica and Juan Figueroa. He first told me that he had learned from Dr. Peñalver, a Venezuelan exile, that Ernesto was safe. The Argentine chargé d'affaires, Sánchez Toranzo, had found him and convinced him to take asylum in his embassy. Ernesto had accepted, but only as a guest; his first plan was to surrender himself in exchange for my freedom. All of our comrades, Peruvians and Venezuelans, as well as Sánchez Toranzo, explained to him that if he did, both of us would be imprisoned; his action wouldn't remedy my situation. They were right, of course. But they had to argue for a long time to convince Ernesto.

The Chilean ambassador, Federico Klein, also came to visit me. The jail administration showed him special consideration and I was allowed to receive him in a private room; the others I had seen from behind bars. Mr. Klein told me that Aramburu, the Peruvian ambassador, had refused to grant me a passport or to intervene for me in any way. I was not surprised to hear this, but it seemed to me an attitude quite unworthy of an ambassador, who is supposedly under the obligation to help and defend the rights of his countrymen. On the other hand, Klein, an ambassador from another country, whom I barely knew, had come to the prison to see me and offer me his help.

The deadline for my hunger strike arrived and I wasn't freed, so I began the strike. I was sent to the infirmary, where they put me to bed, but first I got a haranguing from the warden, who tried everything to make me change my mind. She kept insisting that it was pure madness for a cultured person like myself to hold such ideas. I held my ground.

The warden had a fine dinner sent to me, complete with fancy silverware and napkin. As I looked at it I thought, in the loneliness of the infirmary, "How many days can I resist the temptation to eat food like this?" It was chicken, and its aroma forced me to use all of my willpower to leave it untouched. It stayed there the whole day while I took only occasional sips of water. I thought about the women prisoners I had been teaching.

At eight o'clock in the evening the warden sent for me and told me that the court had agreed to set me free and that I would be questioned the following day. I was greatly surprised; I had resigned myself to a longer stay and was prepared to meet it. It seems that the warden was afraid of what would happen if the strike went on any longer. She knew that I had already gone four days on only tea and apples.

Several articles appeared in the newspapers as a result of statements made by the Red Cross commission; some reporters wanted to interview me, but the warden wouldn't allow it. Nor did I like the idea of being interviewed; it seemed to me that this would be pure exhibitionism.

The next day I was taken to the offices of the attorney general, who accused me of being a Communist because they had found notes on the agrarian reform in Latin America and other parts of the world among my papers. He also charged that I had books on Marxist economics as well as a copy of the labor laws approved and passed by the Arévalo government. Finally, he cited my possession of a pamphlet given out during the Conference for Democracy and Freedom held in Havana in 1950, which Betancourt had organized. Threateningly, the attorney general said to me: "How is it, Miss Gadea, that you do not know that Betancourt is a dangerous Communist?" I found it difficult to keep from laughing in his face. I mention the incident only to indicate the depth of ignorance of the Guatemalans who were taking over the government with the help of North American imperialists.

My reply was simply: "Because, like anyone who knows anything about Latin American politics, I know Betancourt is not a Communist. Quite the contrary, he is the leader of Acción Democrática, which is attempting, like Haya de la Torre, to take power with the support of the bourgeoisie and the blessings of North American imperialists." I added: "It is no crime to possess Marxist literature, a professional must read everything."

He ended the interview by telling me that President Castillo Armas wished to see me. I told him that was all right with me, and the only thing I demanded was a guarantee that I would be able to leave the country and go back to Peru. Four days passed and the order to free me still hadn't been issued. I arranged to send a telegram to Armas demanding to be set free on the basis of my status as a political exile. I also stated that if I wasn't released I would again take up my hunger strike, this time indefinitely.

It was July 26. I remember it distinctly because it is Independence Day in Peru. Around ten o'clock at night, the gates of the prison were opened for me. The common prisoners didn't want me to leave: "Who is going to teach us to read?" I advised them to continue studying on their own. I was really touched: behind those faces hardened by misery, pain, and rough living were the hearts of mothers or sisters, counseling me to take care of myself and return to my parents. Many years have passed and I don't even remember their names, but when I go through difficult moments, I think of them and my spirit is renewed. How many women like them are imprisoned throughout the world, victims of exploitation more than their own failings? And I always arrived at the same conclusion—one must fight to change this system.

After leaving the prison I couldn't go on living with the Mendoza sisters. For the first time in my life I rented an apartment, in a building called San Marcos. The apartment was comfortable but inexpensive. I intended to remain there only fifteen days, at the end of which time I planned to leave Guatemala. I ate in a restaurant owned by a friend. I telephoned Ernesto at the Argentine embassy, and Señora Sánchez Toranzo told me that he wanted to see me and explained what I would have to do to get into the embassy, since there were many policemen surrounding it. I went there the next day and asked for the chargé d'affaires. I had to pass through three sets of guards before getting to the door of the house, only to be told that Sánchez Toranzo had gone out. There was a station wagon filled with soldiers outside the door. I had to go back without seeing Ernesto.

Again he sent a message saying he wished to see me, and not to be afraid to come. Again I tried to enter the embassy, with the same result. It was impossible to get in. It seems the guards thought I was carrying messages or wanted to take asylum; whenever I appeared the police in the station wagon watched me threateningly. Throughout that week Ernesto kept sending me short notes saying how much he wanted to see me. Señora Sánchez Toranzo advised me to tell him not to leave: if he did he would certainly be arrested.

Finally I wrote Ernesto a letter telling him not to rush to leave the country, or at least to wait for the protection of some official guarantee of safe passage. I told him about my application for a passport at the Peruvian embassy being refused.

That week I received a telegram from the presidential palace summoning me for the interview with Castillo Armas that had been one of the conditions for my leaving jail. I had met Armas and his wife before, at the home of a mutual friend, so perhaps, I thought, this might be an extension of courtesy among friends. On the day of the interview I deliberately wore a red dress, and I passed all the checkpoints right up to the reception room door. There, even my handbag was taken from me. I had the impression that the guards thought I might be carrying a bomb.

The man I saw was not the same man, or, rather, didn't seem the same, as the one I had talked with about the Latin American situation. On that occasion he had seemed progressive enough to me. Now even his physical appearance had deteriorated. He looked pale and thin, but with a bulging chest (it was said he wore a bulletproof vest). He greeted me in a friendly manner. He remembered having met me and apologized for my stay in prison. I told him I wanted to leave the country and asked for a guarantee against another arrest since my passport would be delayed: the Peruvian embassy wouldn't issue one without approval from Lima. He promised that the guarantee was forthcoming and told me that if there were any problems I should let him know.

I also asked him to guarantee the same for the other Latin American exiles, as many of them had asked me to take this opportunity to do so. "That," he answered, "will be decided case by case." There was a false note in his voice; it was as if he wasn't free. He didn't talk to me privately; there were two officers by his side, hanging on both his words and mine. He seemed like a puppet, which of course he was: a puppet of Yankee interests and of the oligarchy.

8

TOWARD THE END of August planes arrived from Argentina to pick up the people who had taken asylum in the Argentine embassy. Ernesto's family had sent clothes and some money and suggested that he return with the flight. But he refused and left the embassy without warning.

I had told him of the restaurant where I usually ate in one of my letters, and he appeared there one day while I was having lunch. Everyone in the restaurant carefully ignored him, except for my good friend the owner, who invited him to come and eat anything he liked. And when we walked through the streets downtown after lunch, everyone who knew us looked at us in surprise and was afraid to speak with us; they wouldn't even wave. They obviously thought we were being watched by the police.

Ernesto told me that he had left his passport at the Mexican embassy, where he had applied for a visa, and that he was going to Atitlán for three days. He tried to convince me that I should accompany him to Mexico. I refused. My intention was still to return to Peru, and if I didn't get my passport, I would go to Argentina. He gave me his parents' address so that they might help me if I ended up there.

It is noteworthy that in the midst of this police persecution it occurred to him to visit one of the natural beauties of Guatemala, Lake Atitlán, which is surrounded by twelve small towns bearing the names of the apostles. The inhabitants of these towns speak the

Indian language and wear traditional Indian dress. As always, the desire to expand his knowledge was a driving force, but this trip was also an intelligent way to dodge the police.

That afternoon we went to see Elena de Holst. She had to get rid of all her Marxist and Freudian literature because of the police persecutions, and Ernesto asked her for it. We took the books to Elena's aunt's house; by this time she had calmed down and offered Ernesto a room for the remaining days.

The following day Ernesto left very early, carrying his sleeping bag. He stayed three days in Atitlán, returned, and went to the Mexican embassy to pick up his visa, then came to see me. He was very happy to have seen Lake Atitlán. "If I were not so upset about what has happened in Guatemala," he confessed, "I would have written a poem. One feels like a poet there."

During that trip he observed the people in the country. Quieter and more distrustful than usual, they were aware that changes were taking place, and a mute resistance hovered. "Someday," he said, "these people will rise: they won't be able to forget the revolution or the imperialist attack."

He asked me to help pack the books that he would send to Argentina to his Aunt Beatriz, and after dinner I went over to help him. We had a long discussion about what had happened to us and where we stood.

"I have not insisted lately," he explained, "because, things being the way they are, there is no possibility of starting a new life. But in Mexico we will get married. Have no doubt about it."

I answered, uncertain but happily surprised by his conviction: "Do you really think so? I'm going south . . ."

Then he began to talk about what he was going to do in Mexico. One of his projects was to go into the movie industry. He told me that an old friend of his father's, Ulises Petit de Murat, lived there and was well known in the movie industry. It was true; I had heard his name before. He laughed and added: "It'll remind me of my days in Córdoba and my unrealized artistic ambitions. I'll begin as an extra and later, little by little . . . What do you think?" And, although he was laughing, he insisted that I answer.

At first I had taken all this as a joke, but I knew that sometimes he said things laughingly but actually intended them to be taken seriously. Now I was afraid that he really meant it: after all, he did have the contact in Mexico, his father's friend. Carefully I answered: "I don't think a man like you, with your background and your ideals of justice, can find the means of realizing these ideals in films, except in a country where the revolution is in power. In any capitalist country it would be sheer frustration. You'd be better off with any other job, even cleaning the street. Even as an extra you'd be right in the middle of that ambiance of distorted perspective. Since you've asked for my advice, I say don't do it under any circumstances. If there were a guarantee that you could produce some film you wanted to make—denouncing exploitation, exposing the true problems of society—that would be fine, but not even great actors enjoy that luxury. I believe that you should devote yourself to the medical profession, even if you don't make any money and have to work at something else in order to eat."

He looked at me very somberly and said, very calmly: "All right, I'll consider what you've said. I was just thinking that if life in Mexico were very difficult, I could always resort to this alternative to stay alive."

To this I answered: "In cases of extreme necessity, one can always sweep floors or wash dishes. But you have a profession—practice it."

"Yes," he promised, "I will."

ON REVIEWING THE events of that period it seemed to us that in trying to defend the goals of the Guatemalan people we had become closer than ever. There had been dangerous situations. Ernesto saved many political leaders from persecution after Castillo

Armas' arrival in the capital by finding homes in which to hide them. Among those he hid were the Alfaro sisters from El Salvador. I also knew that he delivered arms.

Naturally we worried about our own respective fates during those moments of danger. But we also thought of each other's safety. When I told Ernesto how I had destroyed the envelope on which I had written his address, he said I had committed an error: in such circumstances one should never write anything down but should memorize it; it was vital to train one's memory.

I told him how grateful I was when I learned of his intention to surrender himself to the police in exchange for my freedom, but repeated that his effort would have been in vain. He answered: "You have been very good to me. Although you could have been arrested on your own account, when I heard that they immediately asked about me at the time of your arrest, I thought perhaps if I surrendered they might release you. But my friends, especially Sánchez Toranzo, wouldn't let me do it."

He went on to tell me about his days in the embassy. At the beginning his status was that of a guest. In the convulsive situation of Guatemala, he could make use of his rights as an Argentinean citizen and, as a guest, could enter and leave the embassy at will. He used this freedom to carry out errands for those in asylum at the embassy, to collect some arms, and to arrange asylum for those in difficult positions or those who wished to leave the country. He played chess, drank maté, and argued politics, always maintaining his position regarding the fight. He read his article about the fall of the Arbenz government to a group that included Cuban Mario Dalmau, and Guatemalan Humberto Pineda, both of whom congratulated him.

Pineda and his brother had also taken asylum in the embassy. We had known Humberto, as Myrna Torres's boyfriend. At that time Myrna was studying in Canada, and she called Humberto one day to see how he was, and sent regards to Ernesto. I remember how Ernesto laughingly described the incident: as an exile, Humberto couldn't answer the phone directly, so it was the ambassador who received Myrna's affectionate words and Ernesto relayed them to Humberto.

Ernesto and the Pineda brothers became good friends. He had long discussions with them, always upholding his theme of struggle, above all for the youth of the land. He inspired them to the point of resolving to escape from asylum—which they eventually did, in the trunk of a car, to join the underground movement.

Ernesto told me how Carlos Pellecer had taken asylum, entering the embassy dressed as a woman. He and Ernesto also had long discussions, Ernesto insisting all the while that the people should have been armed.

Because of his opinions Ernesto became known as a Communist. One day all those considered Communists were separated from the others. There were thirteen, and Ernesto was among them.

OUR ANALYSIS OF what we had experienced in Guatemala led us to the conclusion that the revolution there had failed because popular support was not sought to defend it. Whose fault was it? This would have to be decided in due course by the Guatemalan people. We also concluded that the right way for a revolution to maintain national sovereignty, free of the influence of imperialism, would be for it to arm the people to defend their gains. Many times before we had analyzed faults within the ranks of revolutionaries. It was a whole new process, and the training levels of the revolutionary cadres varied a great deal. There were inevitably bureaucratic excesses. There was sometimes dishonesty in the handling of funds, private business enterprises owned by revolutionary leaders with political positions, and a lack of dynamism was evident in the delayed application of agrarian reform. All of this gave some validity to the reactionary propaganda of the oligarchs and Yankee imperialists. We concluded that an inviolable sense of ethics and the banning of all ownership of private businesses by public officials were indispensable prerequisites for the development of a true revolution.

Moreover, we had seen the active interference of the Church in politics, not only symbolized by an archbishop's marching into the city at the head of the mercenary troops, whose uniforms were adorned with the insignia of the cross, but also in the clandestine rings of Catholics, organized in opposition to the Arbenz government, which played an important role in its downfall.

WHEN HE TOOK me home, Ernesto told me once more that we would be married in Mexico. And once more I laughed: I knew I would be going south. Then he asked me to accompany him partway by train, to Villa Canales, and to return from there. I did so. We hardly spoke along the way. He was so careful and reserved; he held my hand tenderly and recited several poems by César Vallejo. He also recited one he had written for me. I was moved, and for a moment I almost decided to go with him to Mexico. But of course I couldn't without a passport and visa. When the train arrived at Villa Canales, we parted, but up until the last moment he insisted that I should get the necessary documents and come to Mexico. I had given him the addresses of several Peruvians in Mexico, and he said we could easily find each other.

I returned to the capital thinking that I wouldn't see Ernesto again for a long time. True, during the brief trip to Canales I had wanted to go with him, but on the way back, doubts reentered my mind. My thoughts shifted to my projected plans to return to my country or to Argentina.

Back in the capital, as I was leaving the station to go home, I noticed a man on a bicycle; his distinctive features and rough complexion stuck in my mind. I was almost home when I was stopped by two men, one of whom was the man on the bicycle. They asked for my papers, and when I showed them they said that I was under arrest and that I must pick up my things: they were deporting me to Mexico! To a certain degree I was pleased by what was happening; this way, although I had no choice, I would be reunited with Ernesto.

Most of my belongings were in the house of Bauer Paiz, where his sister-in-law was looking after them. The police took me to pick them up. I assumed they would then put me on a plane or train bound for Mexico. To my consternation, they took me to the women's jail. I argued; I demanded a lawyer; I shouted. It made no difference. They told me to wait.

This time in jail I found many leaders of the Alliance for Democratic Women. I immediately tried to organize a general hunger strike, but they paid no attention to me, for their families were sending them very tempting baskets of food. I think if I had remained there longer I could have gotten them to agree to the hunger strike. But I was held only that afternoon and that night. The following morning they took me out and put me on a train bound for Malacatán, on the Mexican border; it was the same train Ernesto had taken. A policeman with a face like a gangster accompanied me.

9

ONCE IN MALACATÁN, I assumed the policeman would put me on a bus and let me cross the border. It was not to be.

I was taken to a small jail, little more than a border-guard post. There were no separate rooms, nor any facilities. There was another prisoner, a former Spaniard who had become a naturalized Argentine. His name was Miguel Fexas; he was about fifty years old, the owner of a restaurant in Amatitlán, jailed merely for having had many officials of the Arbenz government as customers. He told me that he owned a house where he had a lot of valuable furniture and that he was unable to sell even the restaurant. He didn't have a cent on him.

I was greatly relieved to have him there. In a primitive jail, with no guarantee of safety, or any way for my comrades to find me, he was a reassurance. I wasn't mistaken. Time would prove to what degree the presence of Mr. Fexas helped me. In fact, if he hadn't been there on that occasion perhaps I wouldn't be able to tell this story.

I asked the chief of police when I would be permitted to leave for Mexico. He said he didn't know.

The living conditions were terrible, made worse by the sticky heat and insects. I was forced to sleep on a cot in a passageway. I went to bed fully dressed and got up at 5 a.m., hardly having slept at all. There was a very primitive bathroom where I bathed, using a jar to take water from a pail that I had filled from a nearby trough.

No food was brought in. The guard who was assigned to watch us took us to a nearby restaurant where we had to pay for our food. I had to lend money to the Spanish-Argentine.

One night as I lay on my small cot trying unsuccessfully to sleep, I heard laughter and loud talking. The jailer had visitors; one of them was the mayor. They were drinking heavily, and they asked me to drink with them. I refused, firmly telling them that in my position as prisoner I had absolutely no desire to meet anyone, much less drink with them. Let them set me free; then I could behave like a normal individual. My statement disarmed them. They didn't insist, and they didn't bother me again.

One afternoon the head jailer came in carrying a shotgun and asked me to come hunt crocodiles with him along the river. Emphatically, I answered that as a political prisoner I was deprived of my personal rights, that I was very concerned with the arbitrary manner of my imprisonment, and that in such a situation I could hardly consider going on an outing—I had to solve my problem first. He said nothing, his face livid with anger. Then, apparently hoping I would eventually give in, he issued an order that I wasn't to be taken to the restaurant. I accepted the punishment, going without food that day. My attitude must have earned the sympathy of some of the police guards; they offered to mail some letters for me. I accepted immediately. I wrote my Peruvian comrades in exile in Mexico, told them of my situation, and asked them to please arrange asylum for me. I also sent a letter to Ernesto telling him where and in what circumstances I found myself. I told him that he had won, since I was already near Mexico and that as soon as I got the necessary papers, I would join him.

The second-in-command at the jail was a lieutenant, tall, blond, and good-looking. He said he was a nephew of Castillo Armas. He took a liking to me after I rejected his boss's request in front of everyone. Once, when he was taking me to the restaurant to eat, he voiced his disapproval of his boss's behavior; another time, he told me that there was no reason for me to remain in this situation and that he could help me by taking me across the border, but I would have to say that I was his wife. I accepted tentatively but advised him that my fiancé, an Argentine doctor, was waiting for me in Mexico. I also told him that I knew some Peruvian families who would take me in. My mention of the fiancé was only to dispel any intentions he might have toward me; I still wasn't absolutely sure that I would marry Ernesto. He asked me if I could get him a job through one of my contacts in Mexico, since he could not return to Guatemala and face charges for having helped me escape. I suspected that this might be a ploy to identify my Peruvian friends or to discover the whereabouts of the Guatemalan underground cells in Mexico; however, he seemed well intentioned. We agreed that he would find a way to carry out his plan and let me know.

As days passed with no solution to my problem, I began to think about escaping. First, I found out where the Mexican consulate was, and wrote a letter asking for asylum. The houses in this little town were odd: in addition to being of a very lightweight, primitive material, they all had a rear exit. I figured that while I was left alone eating lunch—I had already gained the trust of the guards, simple men who were concerned over the imprisonment of so "friendly and amiable" a lady—I would have time to escape. I only had to run two blocks to reach the Mexican consulate, and by the time they discovered my absence, I would already be in asylum. I planned my escape for the following day, the date that I had established in my letter to the consulate.

That night, however, a courier of Castillo Armas arrived from Guatemala City with orders to expel the Spanish-Argentine and me. We were told the news and were also told that to cross the border without the Mexican guards' catching us would cost fifty *quetzales* each. Mr. Fexas, of course, had no money, and I had only sixty *quetzales*. I told them that we could give twenty each or they would have to wait while I asked for money from friends in Guatemala City or Mexico. I thought that if they didn't accept I could still escape. After an hour of deliberation they accepted; smuggling prisoners across was their private side business.

They took us to a ranch at the edge of the river, trudging through mud. When we arrived, they gave us each a hammock, but sleep was impossible because the clouds of gnats that hovered over us could even penetrate the blankets.

In the still-dark dawn, we were called and taken to the river. There a tall, strong Indian was waiting for us; a middle-aged man who was an excellent swimmer. They all, especially the Indian, showed me great consideration. The Suchiate River was swollen, as it was the end of the rainy season in October, and the current was very strong. I put on a bathing suit while my suitcase was placed in a waterproof plastic bag and tied to a small raft made of logs. I was told by the Indian to hang onto the raft firmly with both hands and to paddle with my feet. He told me that we would be paddling upstream for a stretch. I followed his instructions precisely.

We arrived at the Mexican bank of the river as the sun began to rise over the horizon. We dressed in the bushes. A driver was waiting for us and took us to the home of his sister, married to a laborer in a town called Tapachula.

That evening, the courier who had brought the expulsion orders came to tell us that the orders to set us free had been issued in the capital, and that we were free to return to Guatemala! Of course, I refused to do any such thing, although he insisted that I could demand compensation for the unjust imprisonment to which I had been subjected. I refused emphatically.

Mr. Fexas, however, accepted and went back to Guatemala. He wanted to sell his restaurant and his house. I suspected it was all merely a trick to keep up the smuggling operations. I couldn't say this openly to Mr. Fexas in the presence of the courier, although I did express serious doubts that he would be able to do what he wanted. Afterward I would learn that, in fact, my suspicions were well founded.

I remained in the simple house where I'd been taken. These humble, poor laborers were truly kind and humane to me; their sympathies lay with the Guatemalan Revolution. I began the bureaucratic process of obtaining official asylum, both from the immigration office of Tapachula and directly from Mexico City. I wrote Ernesto and my Peruvian friends telling them that I was already in this Mexican town. The last letter they had received from me must have made them very uneasy.

I was in Mexico, if not in accordance with my plans, at least in accordance with my desires, and Ernesto's. I laughed to myself as I thought how he had been right when he confidently asserted that we would see each other again in Mexico. His predictions had worked out so far, but as for the marriage part, I was still unconvinced. Would that also work out?

Early Guatemala days—an outing at the university campus swimming pool of the capital, December 1953. From left to right: Señora de Temoche, the author, Consuelo España, Ernesto, Gualo García, Señora de Alexander, Ricardo Rojo, and Robert Alexander.

Ernesto before a Mayan carving in Costa Rica.

(Above) Hilda and Ernesto, with his ever-present maté, on a Guatemalan picnic.

(Left) Hilda and Ernesto, during a trip to Toluca.

In Mexico—Ernesto, with guitar, at a birthday party with his General Hospital colleagues.

Ernesto's credential certifying him as an Agencia Latina reporter when he covered the Pan American Games.

A tired, cross, and pregnant Hilda with Ernesto at Chichén Itzá on their honeymoon trip.

A shot of Hilda taken by Ernesto in Veracruz, on their honeymoon.

Armando and Alberto Bayo, flanking an unfamiliar-looking Fidel Castro, in the Mexico City prison yard.

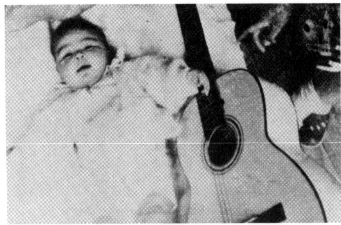

El Patojo snapped this shot of the baby, Hildita, at four months, just after Che had been arrested in Mexico.

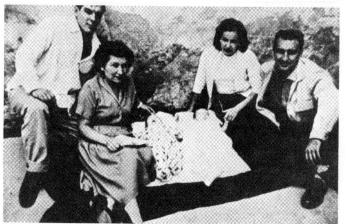

Visitors' day at the prison: the Guevaras, with Hildita on the left, and the Alberto Bayos, with Carmencita on the right.

Che in the foreground of the Cuban prisoners, with María Antonia, in the Miguel Schultz jail.

The June 28 clipping recounts Colonel Bayo's offer to give himself up in exchange for the freedom of Fidel Castro and the others.

The July 11 story covers the detention of Che, Fidel, and García and the expulsion from Mexico of the rest.

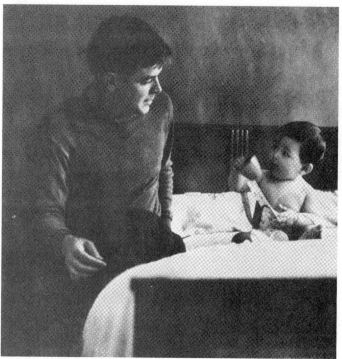

Che playing with his beloved Hildita one weekend before the fateful Granma sailing.

Hilda and the baby arriving in Buenos Airies in January 1957 with Che's parents and sisters; his mother is holding Hildita.

Holed up in Cuba's Sierra Maestra, Che (with his ubiquitous maté) talks to journalist Carlos María Gutiérrez.

Che with Fidel during the uncertain days in the Sierra Maestra.

Things were looking better this day, with Fidel and another fighter, at General Headquarters in La Plata.

After the triumph: Che meeting his parents at Rancho Boyeros airport, Havana, January 1959.

Che, Hilda, and guests at little Hildita's third birthday party, February 15, 1959.

Hildita, photographed by Che in Santiago de las Vegas.

10

ACQUIRING OFFICIAL ASYLUM from Tapachula took a few days. In my application to the local immigration office, I informed the government about how I had entered the country, due to the circumstances I had set out in my first application for political asylum, sent from the jail in Malacatán.

The family that took me in consisted of a husband and wife and their three children, all living in a one-room shack. The father earned fifteen pesos per day—a little more than one dollar—which barely covered the house expenses. Since I still had about twenty *quetzales,* the equivalent of twenty dollars, I changed this money into Mexican currency so that I would be able to share the food expenses. They didn't want to accept, but I insisted. My days with this family were spent mainly strolling through the town, accompanied by the oldest daughter, who was ten or twelve years old at the time.

I sent a cable to my parents asking them for money to cover my trip to Mexico City. Four days later I received a bank draft with sufficient money for my plane ticket and living expenses. I wrote my friends in Mexico City asking them to help me at their end with the Ministry of the Interior, and to tell Ernesto Guevara my whereabouts, in case he hadn't gotten my letter.

I had been in Mexico eight days when a letter came from the interior ministry informing me that I had been granted political asylum and that I could travel to the capital. I immediately sent a telegram to a Peruvian friend, Acosta, asking him to find lodging for me in Mexico City. He was waiting for me at the airport when I arrived, and took me to a hotel called, I think, the Roma. From there I called another Peruvian, Jorge Raygada, but I didn't find him at home. Acosta gave me Ernesto's new telephone number. He had moved and it seemed that indeed he had not received my last letter. I called him immediately and when he answered the phone I covered the mouthpiece with a handkerchief to disguise my voice: "Dr. Guevara?" He immediately recognized my voice, however, and exclaimed: "You're already here! Where are you?" I gave him the name of the hotel and he arrived a few minutes later.

We talked for a long time. I related the details of my departure from Guatemala, and he kept interrupting me with questions. He talked about his train trip and how, after I left him in that town, he had met a young Guatemalan, Julio Roberto Cáceres, whom they called El Patojo on account of his being short, and of how they had become such good friends that they had rented a small apartment together in the center of town. Ernesto was already working in the general hospital in the allergy ward and earning a small salary.

He had also found a way of putting his camera to good use. He had gone into the photography business with Patojo, going around the streets and parks taking pictures of people. Patojo would take care of developing, printing, and selling them to the subjects who had given their addresses to Ernesto.

He asked me to tell him what had happened after I saw him off at the train station up to the time I took the plane to Mexico City from Tapachula. He laughed a little, mocking, as always, but said: "You've lost weight. You've been through quite a bit." I explained that it was due to my worries. He nodded and confessed that he also had been terribly worried about me.

He knew that I had many petty bourgeois prejudices, and he thought the river crossing must have been a really shocking experience for me. He knew of a Spanish woman exile who had undergone the same unfortunate situation and had been badly mistreated by the police. I assured him that crossing the river wasn't that traumatic; there was a certain danger from the strong current, but I was aware of it and knew how to cope with it. But the ruthlessness of the police did make a great impression on me in that, having already received orders to free us, they forced us to leave in a sudden and dangerous way so they could make money by smuggling us across. I told him how Mr. Fexas had gone back to Guatemala immediately, but that I didn't believe that he would succeed in selling his restaurant and house. (A month later I learned that Fexas had been arrested after returning to Guatemala. He escaped and took asylum in the Argentine embassy; he left from there for Mexico without having been able to sell his properties.)

Again Ernesto spoke of the possibility of getting married. I said we should wait. I had just arrived in Mexico and wanted to adjust to the new environment and look for a job. I really was not yet certain. I think he realized this and seemed somewhat bothered by it. I had the feeling that my ambiguous answer had created a certain tension, because he then said that we would just be friends. I was a little surprised: I was only asking him to wait. But I accepted his decision. I had just arrived, and here we were, already quarreling. . . .

At that moment a call came from Comrade Raygada, whom I hadn't been able to reach before. He invited me to lunch the following day and asked me to meet him at the offices of the magazine *Humanismo,* whose editor in chief was Juan Juarbe y Juarbe. The appointment was for one o'clock in the afternoon. When I put the phone down Ernesto said: "Okay. You already have an invitation. I can't invite you out now, but we'll go out sometime."

The important thing in our first meeting in Mexico lay in a question he suddenly asked: "Do you think the Communists should fight in a revolution for the rights of the people?"

I looked at him and thought, Well now, what is this? Could it be that he's already seen the Cubans? Is he with comrades from other countries or is he thinking of his own?

Putting aside my questions, I gave him my frank opinion: "I believe the Communists should be at the vanguard of the struggle for the rights of the people. In a revolution the Communists must always be at the forefront."

He listened attentively and then said: "Yes. I think so, too."

I felt as if he was promising something. I tried to figure out whether he had said this on account of the quarrel we had just had or if he was really committed. Then, knowing him as well as I did, I realized that he would have said the same thing even if I had agreed to marry him immediately.

He left hurriedly, saying that he had to help develop some film that had to be delivered the following day and that he had to get up very early to go to the hospital. He promised to phone me in the morning to find out what time he could see me.

Later in the evening, my friend Acosta came see how I was making out. We discussed the possibility of finding a boarding-house; it would be less expensive and I would feel more at ease.

The first time I left the hotel I went to visit some Venezuelan exiles, among them Comrade Dascoli. I had worked with him in Guatemala, and he was now working for the ECLA (Economic Commission for Latin America). I wanted to say hello to him and also to discuss work possibilities for me. Dascoli treated me very kindly: "Hilda, if you need money or anything let us know. We're worried about you and so are the Peruvian comrades." There was one Peruvian working in ECLA, Tejada, who reiterated the offer. I thanked them and explained that my parents had sent me enough money to live for two or three months in Mexico.

Dascoli told me that he knew a Venezuelan girl who was also in exile. She was single and her name was Lucila Velásquez, a poet.

He suggested that we might get together and perhaps share living quarters. We made a date for that same afternoon.

I met and liked Lucila Velásquez. The fact that we were both in exile and both alone drew me closer to her. We both moved to a boardinghouse near the Paseo de la Reforma for a place to stay while searching for an apartment. I gave Ernesto my new address, and he came to the boardinghouse from time to time to visit me, but he had no opportunity to meet Lucila until later, when we both moved to an apartment.

It was on the occasion of that early November lunch with Raygada, just after I arrived in Mexico City, that I met Luis de la Puente. When I arrived at the offices of the magazine *Humanismo*, which was put out by Raúl Roa, Juan Juarbe y Juarbe, and Ildegar Pérez Segnini (a Venezuelan exile I had met in Guatemala), Raygada and Juarbe were already there. They introduced me to Puente, who told me that he was returning to Peru shortly.

After lunch we all went to visit Señora Laura de Albizu Campos, a distinguished Peruvian, whom I wanted very much to meet because I knew of her activities and her dedication to the cause of Puerto Rico. She lived in Lomas de Chapultepec, in the rear of a house where she sublet a small apartment.

Doña Laura told me about the struggle in Puerto Rico, the revolution in 1950, how she met her husband, Don Pedro, and what this great patriot had done for the liberation of Puerto Rico. She was convinced that the Yankees were not going to release him, because he represented the most coherent point of view within the revolutionary struggle of Puerto Rico and the continent. She spoke to me worriedly about the torture to which her husband was subjected daily, about how much his health had suffered. She was convinced that the Yankees would never let him go, that they were going to kill him. (In fact, in 1964, completely paralyzed and unable to speak, Pedro Albizu Campos was released, only to die. Such was the extent to which the imperialists persecuted this patriot, champion of national sovereignty.)

Luis de la Puente also greatly impressed me, with his strong personality, his preoccupation with Peruvian problems, and his constant protest against the exploitative, miserable conditions of our country. He briefed me on the state of the Committee of Aprista Exiles in Mexico. He explained how there were two factions within the committee; the orthodox group, which rigidly followed the party line of the Aprista Party, and the other, representing the true revolutionary element, of which he was a part. The latter faction included poet Gustavo Valcarcel and a group of young people who would later be expelled from APRA and join the Communist Party. Puente told me how Haya de la Torre himself called him on his way through Mexico, and after a disciplinary talk succeeded in getting Puente to return to the Committee of Exiles, from which he had been expelled. Speaking about the Peruvian situation—this was toward the end of 1954 and the presidential elections in Peru were coming up—Puente explained to me that a coalition was in the making between APRA and the reactionary forces represented by one of the pillars of the banking industry in Peru, the Prado family. He, of course, didn't agree, and, like many other young people, thought we shouldn't, under any circumstances, accept the party line and vote for Prado: what should be done was to make revolution. With this aim, he said, he was returning to Peru, where he would join a group of comrades that was waiting for him.

A few days later, Raygada, Juarbe, and I gave a farewell party for Puente in the home of Doña Laura, who also thought highly of him. Despite the fact that we knew Luis de la Puente, "Lucho," was going to Peru to join a soon-to-begin struggle, it was a joyful occasion. Lucho sang a few songs in Quechua, the Peruvian Indian tongue, and the party was a success. Ironically, we ended up singing prison songs.

I had thought about introducing Ernesto to Puente and the rest of the group, but the strain in our relationship persisted from the day he announced that we would be only friends, and an opportunity never arose. Puente departed without having met Ernesto, to my regret. A month later I would learn that Puente had been arrested attempting to enter Peru; his group had been betrayed by an informer.

WHILE I WAS living in the boardinghouse with my friend Lucila, Ernesto did call me two or three times to invite me out to eat or to go to the museum or the movies. He told me that he had learned of my whereabouts through Acosta, for whom I had given Ernesto a letter of introduction when he left Guatemala. He appreciated the fact that I had undergone difficulties and regretted that he was unable to spare me the ordeal. He then told me how he had become friends with El Patojo, whom he loved like a son. He had gotten Patojo a job as a night watchman at a publishing firm, and sometimes Ernesto substituted for him.

When I told Ernesto that I had written to his former address on Bolívar Street, he decided we should go there to get the letter. We did, and found it, but when I asked him to give it back to me since our relationship had changed, he refused and proceeded to read it. This was a letter in which I rebuked him for not writing, but he assured me that he had sent a letter to Señora de Toriello's house and that I would surely receive it eventually; he had just written to Guatemala asking them to forward my mail.

During the last week of November he invited me to the movies. The Soviet ballet version of *Romeo and Juliet* was playing, and we both enjoyed it immensely. Later we sat down and discussed the universality of Shakespeare, whose works we both knew. That evening we made up.

Toward the beginning of December, Lucila and I found an apartment. We split the expense of buying cheap furniture, and we moved in immediately. Ernesto continued to visit me frequently and eventually he met Lucila.

Ernesto used to come by the house in the afternoons. One day he told me how he had gotten his job in the hospital: A Central American woman doctor had introduced him to the head of the general hospital in Mexico, Dr. Salazar Mayen, who offered him a position as assistant in the allergy ward, his specialty. He added that the job paid very little, but that it allowed him to practice medicine. One day just before I arrived, that is, toward the end of October, Ñico López came into the ward with another Cuban, who was suffering from allergy. Ernesto and Ñico embraced each other, friends reunited. Ñico told him that they had many projects under way: they were in constant contact with Cuba, with the groups from the 26th of July Movement, and they expected that soon Fidel, Raúl, and other comrades would soon be let out of jail.

At this point the various groups of the 26th of July had no unifying structure; they were made up of people close to Fidel, whose militancy was mostly aimed at getting other organizations and prominent people to join their struggle to free the Moncada fighters. Ñico had high hopes that Fidel would be released and be able to continue revolutionary activities. By the time I arrived, Ñico was in Cuba, but Ernesto said he would bring him over when he came back.

I was very happy to receive news of a good friend and to learn that he kept in touch with his comrades in exile throughout Latin America. They all intended to get together in Mexico, where the ties with Cuban groups were direct. I was also happy that Fidel and the others might be freed soon.

It was then that I understood why Ernesto had asked me that question concerning whether the Communists should fight in a revolution.

11

WE SPENT THE month of December in harmony. Sometimes Ernesto ate with us. He would entertain us with the daily stories from the hospital and his activities as a street photographer. The comments of the people he photographed were sometimes amusing, as was Patojo's failure to deliver photographs on time, thereby losing clients. Ernesto took it all in stride; he could see the humor in it. He said he had continued to record his observations in his diary and that he expected to organize it one day.

Ernesto had also run into Alfonso Bauer Paiz, who had been the minister of economics and a good friend of ours. Bauer Paiz had been very surprised to find Ernesto taking pictures in the park. He invited him to the restaurant he was managing at the time, and told him what had happened to him and his family from the time they took asylum in the Mexican embassy in Guatemala.

My mail was forwarded from Guatemala and I found the letter Ernesto had sent, in which he wrote of his arrival in Mexico City, meeting the Central American doctor and the director of the general hospital, and of his job in the allergy ward. He also wrote that he contacted his father's friend, the movie man Ulises Petit de Murat, who received him very well and invited him to his house. Murat's daughter was very charming, and they served great meals in their house. He ended with a joke: "Come soon, because between the daughter and the beefsteaks, something's going to happen."

We laughed, and somehow reading that letter reinforced our reconciliation. I understood then that he had thought of me all the time I had remained in Guatemala and that he had sincerely wanted me to come to Mexico soon.

All during the month of December I was busy trying to get the necessary working permit. I went daily to the Ministry of the Interior and used whatever time I had left to meet with other exiles or to visit museums or nearby archaeological ruins.

The times Ernesto and I spent together were delightful. Sometimes he discussed poetry with Lucila, but mostly we discussed Latin American politics and also the Mexican Revolution, so much admired throughout our continent, a revolution that we now had a chance to witness firsthand. Unfortunately we could see that there was strong foreign pressure on the PRI (Institutional Revolutionary Party, the political party of the government) and that there still existed a large, cumbersome bureaucracy in public administration. The great aims of the Mexican Revolution had not been attained; the peasant did not possess the land. It is true that some banks extended credit, which unfortunately went more often to the wealthy farmer than to the poor peasant. We were aware that it was very difficult to change the situation because, under the auspices of the PRI, a national bourgeoisie had developed. Closely tied to the interests of the imperialists, this class wanted no change in the structure.

All over the world Christmas is celebrated by large dinners. We prepared to have one at our house and invited Ernesto and Patojo. But Patojo couldn't come because he was working, and Ernesto arrived late because he had to stop by María Antonia's house to say hello to the Cubans and then swing by his house to pick up his sleeping bag. He meant to keep Patojo company on his watchman's job. Ernesto had to leave before midnight. I fixed up some of the Christmas dinner for him to take to Patojo, along with a small present that I had gotten him, and then I gave Ernesto his present, a brown sweater. He laughed at my disappointment over his not being able to stay until midnight: "What's this passion that women have for celebrating holidays? The last thing I need is for you to make a scene because I can't stay." He added, smiling: "It's not so bad, I'll come by tomorrow and we can go out together."

Ernesto's late arrival and Patojo's not being able to come had ruined Lucila's mood. I, in turn, was disappointed because I had passed up an invitation to a party with my Peruvian friends to be with Ernesto and Patojo. Wanting to cheer me up, Lucila urged me to accompany her to a party at the house of a Venezuelan family, but I declined, thinking about Ernesto's promise to come by the next day.

The next morning he appeared around 10 a.m. and we went out. We spent a beautiful day in Chapultepec Park. Ernesto wore the new sweater I had given him.

"I owe you a present," he said. "I had no time to pick one out."

LUCILA INVITED US to a New Year's Eve party with the Venezuelans, but Ernesto could not go. He ate with us early that evening, and between 9 and 10 p.m. said he had to go meet Patojo, who was working.

I interpreted his quick departure as a lack of interest in me, and I decided to end our engagement then and there. I told him, but he wouldn't believe it. I declared that I was going to the party given by the Venezuelans. He said this was fine; no problem—I should go with Lucila. This hurt me even more. I felt I was being treated very indifferently by Ernesto, and my sense of self-respect wouldn't tolerate it. New Year's is usually spent with loved ones, and we were both away from our families. To me it seemed logical that we should be together. Instead Ernesto preferred to be with Patojo. I went off to the party firmly resolved to break with Ernesto.

At the party I met a Venezuelan poet, also in exile, who was very attentive. Feeling that my relationship with Ernesto was over, and to strengthen my resolve, I danced most of the night with the

Venezuelan. He asked me to go out with him next day, promising that if I accepted he would come with a Venezuelan couple to pick me up. I almost decided to accept his offer and go out with him—just as a friend, of course—but with the intention of getting to know him better, as his manner and conversation were interesting.

The following day, around nine o'clock in the morning, very early considering it was New Year's Day, I was surprised to see Ernesto arrive. He had come to take me out. All of my resentment of the previous day evaporated, and we made up. We then went all the way to Toluca for the day, very happy to be starting the new year together.

Later on Ernesto brought me a New Year's present. I remember that we had a slight disagreement that day, but later he came to eat with us. After lunch he handed me a small green leatherbound volume. It was an edition of José Hernández's "Martín Fierro," the poem from which he so often used to recite verses, applying them to some event in our lives, to the reality in which we lived. "Read the inscription," he said. I opened the book. On the flyleaf it said: "To Hilda, so that on the day we part the substance of my hopes for the future and my predestined struggle will remain with you. Ernesto 20–1–55."

I was very moved. I tried to hide my emotion.

He stayed for some time that day. Eventually Lucila left the room and we turned to more personal matters, the disagreement completely forgotten. I confessed that I had been deeply moved by what he had written in the book.

"Yes, I noticed," he said. "You cried a little but, being stubborn, you tried to hide it. However, I know you better than you know yourself. I had wanted to give it to you on New Year's Day, but I didn't have the money at the time. It doesn't matter, does it?"

IN THE NEW YEAR I took an intensive course on the Mexican Revolution at the university, while I was waiting for a work permit. The course lasted for two months and was well worth the time. Many professors, economists, and sociologists participated. I met some fellow students, graduates from different faculties, especially economics and philosophy, and had interesting discussions with them on the various lectures. Basically the course, employing accurate statistics, demonstrated the fact that the aims of the Mexican Revolution had not been attained, and that furthermore, through the years, Yankee capitalist penetration had intensified.

I discussed all this with Ernesto. In addition we read books on the Mexican Revolution, like John Reed's *Insurgent Mexico,* the memoirs of Pancho Villa, and others.

ERNESTO KEPT INSISTING from time to time that we should marry. I was more open to the idea, but I still harbored doubts. One day, feeling pressured, and perhaps because I was really trying to arrive at a decision, I asked him: "What would this mean to you?"

He looked at me and calmly replied: "Well, it would be completeness. There is so much intelligence, comradeship, love, everything."

I was convinced. I decided to accept. I said we should get married the following March, exactly one year since we became real friends in Guatemala, when he was sick.

He laughed and said: "You and your dates. Why does it have to be exactly a year after? It could be now, it could be at the end of the month. Why does it have to be March?"

"Well," I answered, "let's just let it be."

After one evening's visit he forgot to take the little Einstein book that we were translating. I began to reread sections and was surprised to find a photo negative among the pages. I held it up to the light and discovered that it was a picture of a girl in a bathing suit. I didn't know who it was, but it certainly wasn't me. Next morning I put it in an envelope and sent it with a note telling Ernesto the engagement was off, we would just be friends.

He came over that afternoon despite the fact that he had told me the evening before that he wouldn't have time. He explained that the girl in the picture was Petit de Murat's daughter, who was engaged; the picture had been taken before I arrived in Mexico and it meant nothing. He said that I was using it as an excuse to not marry him, and if that were the case he could only accept, but we couldn't even be friends.

I didn't think he meant it, but a week went by without his coming to see me. Things became even more complicated; it was becoming terribly cold in Mexico City—two or three degrees below freezing—and I was used to the eternal spring of Guatemala. Located on the ground floor of the building, our apartment was very damp, and although the building was new, humidity stained the walls. We were forced to look for a warmer apartment, and in the meantime, we bought a small heater and many blankets. None of this did much good, and finally with the humidity and the cold I came down with a severe case of grippe, aggravated by an acute ear infection.

By the time we had moved to a new apartment in Colonia Cuahutémoc, I was confined to bed with a high fever, a sharp pain in my ear, and a sore throat that prevented me from speaking. Lucila, who cared for me like a sister, was greatly worried about my health and decided to get Ernesto. She knew we had broken up, but she went anyway. She didn't find him at home but reached him at the hospital.

Ernesto came and examined me. "Actually," he said, "you have acute tonsillitis complicated by an ear infection." He gave me an antibiotic and told me that I had to continue the treatment. He said he couldn't see me frequently because he was very busy at the hospital, but left a prescription, and said that he would come to see me in a week. If the fever didn't go down I was to call a throat specialist.

While he was there, he told me of a chance meeting with an Argentine doctor, Alfonso Pérez Vizcaíno, who was then director of the Latin News Agency, financed by Perón to obtain and distribute news directly. They had talked at length and a friendship ensued. This doctor was of course surprised to find a colleague working as a street photographer, but Ernesto explained that he also practiced his profession at the general hospital.

At that time the Pan American Games were underway in Mexico City. The news agency had to report the games and, in order to help Ernesto, the director hired him to assist with the coverage. So Ernesto worked as a news photographer after his shift at the hospital. He got the Cubans to develop the pictures so they, too, could make some money. The work was done in the Cubans' apartment, near mine.

Ernesto's treatment worked, and a week later, recovered and back on my normal schedule, I decided that, since I missed Ernesto and wanted to make up, I should take the initiative. Myrna Torres and her family were now in Mexico. She had married her friend Humberto Pineda, and as before, she invited me to her house often. I asked her to accompany me to visit the Cubans' house; I knew that Ernesto was frequently there developing pictures. So we went one afternoon and found them all working together. I was introduced to a Cuban who, from the moment I arrived, kept up a barrage of gallantries and typical Cuban pick-up lines, including asking me repeatedly to marry him. Ernesto enjoyed it, laughing at the jokes, and when we said goodbye, he said, "Are you going to be home tomorrow? I'll come to see you."

At home the next day, he promptly asked me whether I had made up my mind. His tone was calm but firm. It sounded like an ultimatum.

I really was decided. "Yes," I said. "We will be married in May." That was two months off, and first we would have to get the government's permission and put our papers in order. We knew that there was a good deal of red tape involved, but we didn't realize how complicated it was going to be.

Later I asked him if he thought I would say yes. He replied very seriously: "Yes, because you knew you'd lose me this time if you said no."

He said the Cubans had teased him after I left, saying: "Hilda came; now you're happy, Che." They knew that we had quarreled.

Laughing, he added that the Cuban who had been flirting with me had apologized to him after the others told him I was Ernesto's girl. He had told the Cuban not to worry, there was no problem; we were on the outs. "Besides," he said, "I was sure of you; that's why I could laugh."

This Cuban was to become Ernesto's good friend, and after we were married he came to visit us several times. He was a barber and he taught Ernesto how to cut hair; Ernesto was practicing in the hospital. When I asked him why, his answer was: "Everything you learn is useful and can someday come in handy, don't you think?"

Doña Laura fell ill, and one day I took Ernesto to see her. On that occasion I introduced him to Juarbe and to another Puerto Rican who lived with him. Ernesto gave Doña Laura a thorough examination and a prescription that he subsequently took to her himself, explaining that if she went to the hospital to get it, it would cost less but it would involve a long delay. They talked about Puerto Rican problems and the situation of Don Pedro. I had already told Ernesto about all this and had read him several of the publications on the torture suffered by the Puerto Rican patriots in jail. Ernesto had thought that these publications had exaggerated a bit. However, after listening to Doña Laura he came to share our fear that Don Pedro would be killed.

Doña Laura, Juarbe, and Ernesto hit it off so well that from then on we went there once a week, and on these occasions we would go over the problems and events in Latin America. They analyzed several countries; we told them of the Guatemalan situation. These meetings were always productive, invariably reaffirming our conclusion that our struggle in Latin America was against Yankee imperialism.

I had been to see a specialist in agricultural economics, Don Ramón Fernández y Fernández, who had been in Guatemala for a conference on controlled credits, at which I had the opportunity to work with him and Alfonso Rocha. Dr. Fernández recommended me to Dr. Urquidi, director of ECLA, where they needed someone to write a report on coffee for El Salvador. I was fortunate enough to get the position, which was to last three months. As it turned out I worked for only two months because in May there was an opening available for a statistician at the Pan American Health Office, a branch of the World Health Organization. A Peruvian friend, Tejada, told me about it; I applied and got the job. This made a great deal of difference in getting my permit, since I could go to the Ministry of the Interior with a concrete job offer, whereupon they granted me the legal authorization for which I had petitioned so eagerly.

Meanwhile, we continued to make arrangements for our marriage. We kept running into new problems. I remember that once a high official, talking to the undersecretary, whom I had finally gotten to see after a month of daily visits, said: "Imagine—this lady is a Peruvian exile and she wants to marry an Argentine."

I almost laughed in their faces. I thought of telling them that they couldn't force me to marry a Mexican just to avoid legal problems. Instead I said, docilely, "Yes, that is the situation. I hope you can resolve it."

The month of May arrived, however, and we were still waiting for the papers.

Previously we had agreed on March, and it was I who broke the agreement. Now I had made another promise to Ernesto, and I couldn't break this one. Besides, we had made reservations for a weekend in Cuernavaca.

So we decided to live together, leaving the formality of signing the papers for whenever we could get the authorization.

WE HAD TAKEN part in the May Day parade in Guatemala during the time of the Arbenz government, so we wanted to be present at the Mexico City festivities to compare them.

Ricardo Rojo had come back April 30. Ernesto said we would meet him on the morning at the Independence Monument to see the parade. He told me that Rojo had asked about me, how things were going with us, and if we were planning on getting married. He had told him that we were but that we didn't know when.

May 1 was sunny. We met Rojo and found a good vantage point from which to see the parade. It wasn't very impressive. There was a fairly large number of participants, but it was obvious that the workers weren't exactly expressing the victories of the class struggle. They were there merely to fulfill a routine. They seemed more fiesta-minded than conscious of the day's importance or the meaning of a proletarian demonstration.

Suddenly I spied a familiar face and I called out: "Look! There's Fortuny." It was the same José Manuel Fortuny who had been secretary-general of the Communist Party of Guatemala and had played one of the main roles in the last events before Guatemala fell before the imperialistic attack.

Rojo said, "Why don't you call him over? Let's talk to him." Ernesto nodded. "Yes. We can ask him what happened in Guatemala. Why they didn't fight."

I called Fortuny over and introduced them all. At last Ernesto was meeting him, after trying unsuccessfully for months in Guatemala. After the usual greetings, we asked him the question.

Fortuny looked somewhat surprised, and, appearing unsure of himself, he answered, "We saw the situation as very difficult, and decided we should abandon the government to continue fighting from the plains. The fight will continue—we're trying to keep it going."

We were dumbfounded by this preposterous explanation. Finally Ernesto spoke: "Well, comrade, perhaps it would have been better to fight while you had power in your hands. It might have been different."

"What do you mean?" asked Fortuny, in a near-hostile tone. "Exactly what I said," replied Ernesto. "If President Arbenz had left the capital to go into the interior with a group of true revolutionaries, the outlook would have been different. His status as constitutionally elected president would have made him a symbol and a great moral force. The chances of remaking the revolutionary government would have been much better."

Fortuny was silent; the argument had hit home. We said goodbye perfunctorily.

Later we talked about it. Fortuny's answer still seemed incredible. "That was just an excuse," Ernesto said. "There are many advantages when one fights from a position of power, but whether with power or without, the only course there was to fight."

Rojo nodded in agreement, but his anti-Communist feelings cropped up when he laughed and said: "You are taking advantage of the circumstances to bring out your vehemence for the destruction of the established system. It's not quite like that. It's true that one has to fight for the people's welfare, but within the known framework of democracy, respecting the prevailing principles, and not imposing foreign ideas favoring only one ideological group."

The discussion, bitter at times, went on between them for quite a while, while I thought about everything that had happened that morning. A few days later Rojo left Mexico. He said he would write us and, if he ever came through again, he would stop in for a visit.

On June 14 we celebrated Ernesto's birthday at home. We had a small party, to which we invited the Torres family, a Peruvian couple, and a woman from Costa Rica. Don Edelberto Torres Jr. told

Ernesto about a trip to China that was being organized for which one had to pay only part of the passage. The next day Ernesto talked about the trip. We calculated our available resources. Between us we could hardly come up with the three hundred dollars for one to go.

Trying to conceal my disappointment, I said: "All right, you're going. When do you leave?" He realized what I was thinking. "If you don't go, neither of us goes," he said. "Anyhow, we're going to get married. I only wanted to know what you thought. I'll thank Don Edelberto and we'll go some other time. I'll keep on trying for the marriage permit, and if we can't go to a judge, we'll go to an embassy."

"All right," I answered, "we'll go to the Peruvian one."

"No," he protested, "we'll go to the Argentine."

The Torres family was very surprised that Ernesto would pass up an opportunity like that. They would only understand why when we were married.

12

SHORTLY AFTER WE returned from Cuernavaca, Ernesto came home one night with Raúl Castro. Raúl's spontaneity and cheerful and easy manner led to a strong friendship. Conversation with Raúl was very interesting. Despite his youth—he was twenty-three or twenty-four years old at the time—and his even younger appearance, blond and beardless and looking like a university student, his ideas were very clear as to how the revolution was to be made and, more important, for what purpose and for whom. He had great faith in Fidel, not because he was his brother but because of his political leadership. It was his faith in Fidel that had led him to participate in the Moncada attack. He was convinced that in Cuba, as in most of Latin America, one could not expect to take power through elections: armed struggle was necessary. But this effort must be carried out in close union with the populace; power would come only with the support of the people. With this, one could go on to transform the capitalist society into a new, socialist society. Raúl held Communist ideas; he was a great admirer of the Soviet Union and had participated in the Youth Festival of Stockholm in 1952. He firmly believed that the power struggle must benefit the people, and that this struggle against imperialism was not only for Cuba, but for all of Latin America.

He promised to bring Fidel to our house as soon as he arrived in Mexico. From then on he came to our house at least once a week, and Ernesto saw him almost every day. He had already been introduced to some of our exile friends. Raúl always gave us the latest news from Cuba: we learned that Fidel was on his way; that Ñico could not yet return to the capital and had to remain in Veracruz; that he was going to Cuba. He also told us how they had begun to organize the 26th of July Movement. Moreover, it was spirit-lifting just to talk to him: joyful, communicative, sure of himself, and very clear in his ideas, he had an incredible capacity for analysis and synthesis. That is why he understood Ernesto so well.

Toward the beginning of July, Ernesto told me that Fidel was in Mexico City, and that he had met him at the home of María Antonia, a Cuban married to a Mexican, who lived at Number 49 Emparán. They had talked for almost ten straight hours—from eight o'clock at night to the following morning. Fidel, he said, was a new type of great political leader—modest, but he knew where he wanted to go, and he had tenacity and firmness. They had spent the time exchanging ideas on the Latin American and international scenes. We knew that Fidel had a deep faith in Latin America. We had also learned from Ñico in Guatemala that Fidel had been in Colombia at the time Gaytan was murdered and that he wanted to fight alongside the Colombians. That is another quality that Ernesto discovered in Fidel—his being a true Latin American, a profound admirer of the ideas of José Martí, an inspiration for all Cubans. He also found in Fidel a deep conviction that in fighting against Batista, he was fighting the imperialist monster that kept Batista in power.

He concluded: "Ñico was right in Guatemala when he told us that if Cuba had produced anything good since Martí it was Fidel Castro. He will make the revolution. We are in complete agreement. . . . I could only fully support someone like him."

Ernesto said that since that first day he had been meeting with Fidel three or four times a week. He had stopped keeping a record in his diary as a precaution. The Cubans were being harassed, and he would not be surprised if one day they were jailed—it wasn't only the Batista police that were after them but also the FBI.

One night Ernesto announced: "Fidel is coming tomorrow. Let's host a dinner for him and invite Doña Laura and Juarbe."

We had the dinner. Lucila, of course, was also there. But Fidel was late and Lucila got tired of waiting and went up to her room. When Fidel finally arrived we talked with him for a while and then called Lucila to come down and meet him and perhaps read some of her poetry, which was about to be published. Lucila, however, couldn't be talked into coming down. "You'll see my poetry when it's published," she called down from her room. The following week Fidel came again and he finally met Lucila.

It was certainly very impressive to personally meet this student leader who, on July 26, 1953, had led a group of workers and students in an attack on the Moncada Barracks. He was young, only thirty, fair-skinned, and tall, about six foot two, and solidly built. His wavy hair was deep black and shiny, and he had a mustache. His movements were quick, agile, sure. He did not look like the leader one knew him to be. He could very well have been a handsome bourgeois tourist. When he talked, however, his eyes shone with passion and revolutionary zeal, and one could see why he could command the attention of listeners. He had the charm and personality of a great leader, and at the same time an admirable simplicity and naturalness. I remember well how his insistence that Lucila should come down, and the deep respect he showed for Doña Laura, broke the ice that night. We were all in awe of him, except Ernesto, who had already spoken with him at length.

Fidel asked about the Puerto Rican situation, giving both Juarbe and Doña Laura a chance to explain it, and then showing his own knowledge and conviction (shared by all Cubans from Martí on), he said that Puerto Rico should fight for complete sovereignty, without minimizing the difficulties in the fact that the territory was practically a Yankee colony.

Juarbe expounded on the cultural richness of Puerto Rico and its folklore, little known in the other Latin American countries. Later on, we talked about Peru and the rest of our continent.

Overcoming my awe, I dared to ask him: "So tell us, why are you here when your place is in Cuba?"

He answered: "Very good question. I'll explain."

His answer lasted four hours, during which he made an exhaustive analysis of the situation in his country and the difficult reasons that kept him from being there.

In the first place, he said, he could not remain in Cuba because he was being watched by the Batista police. He believed that there was no hope in elections, as some other political leaders maintained, that the only alternative was to fight directly for power. Elections were a masquerade. If nothing concrete was done, they'd have Batista for forty years. One must prepare for the fight; no matter how long it might last it was the only solution. Cuba was becoming more and more corrupt each day. Yankee penetration was complete. The spirit of the Moncada attack had to be kept burning with an armed struggle that would little by little raise the masses. Although Moncada had failed, much had been learned from the defeat, and the experience would be useful in the new strikes. He had come to Mexico to train a group of fighters to invade and openly confront the Batista army supported by the Yankees and call on the people to join him. In order to do all this, he had to evade capture.

He went on to tell us of the methods that would be employed in this new venture: training men for combat; organizing the movement; setting up support committees in the country as well as abroad; distributing tasks; and establishing security measures to ensure the utmost secrecy (there would always be infiltrators, but with proper security these could be detected in time). The security measures would apply to men as well as arms and orders. In this they had already had positive experience in planning and executing the Moncada attack and they would intensify it.

Lastly, he explained that the struggle in Cuba was part of the continental fight against the Yankees, a fight that Bolívar and Martí had foreseen.

When Fidel ended his discourse, I was absolutely convinced and ready to accompany them. But I didn't say anything. I decided to await a better opportunity. Later, I asked Ernesto if Fidel would take women. He looked at me and understood immediately what I meant: "Perhaps women like you—but it would be very difficult. Why don't you talk with him?"

But I never had the chance.

I do remember very well that a few days later, as we were discussing the future, Ernesto asked me very seriously: "What do you think of this crazy idea of the Cubans, invading an island completely defended by coastal artillery?"

I realized perfectly well that he was asking my opinion as to whether or not he should participate in the expedition. I knew the risk that our separation would mean and the tremendous danger involved. Yet, aware of all this, honestly and out of conviction, I said: "There is no doubt. It is crazy, but one must go along."

Embracing me, he said, "I agree, but I wanted to know what you'd say. I have decided to join the expeditionary force. We are only at the planning stage, but we'll begin training soon. I will go as a doctor." Our destiny was thus sealed with pain and happiness at the same time—pain because of the risks, happiness because we were contributing in a small way to the liberation of our continent.

ONE DAY SOMETHING happened that made me realize to what degree Ernesto was aware that the Cubans were being persecuted and how much he considered both of us to be part of their group. We still lived in the apartment with Lucila. (We were still waiting for the marriage permit and considering a bribe for the speedy processing of our papers. Of course, paying it was impossible since it went against our revolutionary principles, and besides, we could not have afforded that large sum.) We were already looking for another apartment. One afternoon when I came back from work I found our room in disarray. I noticed that the typewriter, Ernesto's camera, some of his medical instruments, and a few pieces of jewelry that I had were missing. We had been robbed; there was no doubt about it. When Lucila arrived we agreed to wait until Ernesto came home, and when he did, we showed him the room without saying anything. At first he didn't understand what had happened. "Didn't you have time to straighten up the room?" he asked. "Did you get here very late after work?"

"No, this is the way I found it," I replied. Later he said: "There's no doubt, this is the work of the FBI. We can't tell the police. Even if it weren't a fake robbery, we wouldn't have the things returned to us."

So we didn't report the theft. I doubted very much that we would have recovered anything, and besides, it would have been a great bother. We were especially sorry to lose some of our things. I had been helping him type his work on the doctors in Latin America. He would have to go for a long time without a camera; fortunately he was not using it to take pictures in the street anymore; he had left the job entirely in Patojo's hands because he was too busy. He had begun work in an allergy lab where he was preparing the defense of his dissertation in physiology, which he eventually passed.

We were forced to buy another typewriter on credit, although we were still paying for the previous one. Ernesto had written a paper on allergy to be presented at a congress in Veracruz in September 1955, and I had to type it. Also, I helped him to compile the statistical data and figure out averages. According to him, I had helped a great deal, in lengthy discussions, to clarify his conclusions. His work was selected to appear in the *Journal of Allergy*. He gave me one copy and wrote at the top of the first page: "With love, to Hilda, who has been my guide and stimulus, and without whose help I could not have reached my conclusions or finished this work." Unfortunately I lost the copy of the magazine when I left Mexico, when many of the packages of books I sent to Lima never arrived.

By September, Ernesto was invited to present his paper to the Congress on Allergy at Veracruz, but since I couldn't accompany him, he didn't go.

THE PROPOSAL TO organize a movement centered around Fidel Castro, to continue with the struggle that had begun with the abortive attack on the Moncada, was already generally accepted among the Cubans. They organized a ceremony with other Latin Americans, especially Venezuelans and Peruvians, in front of the Martí statue in Chapultepec Park to commemorate the first 26th of July that they were spending out of jail.

I couldn't attend because, if I remember correctly, the ceremony was to be held during working hours, but Ernesto took me later to the apartment of the Jiménez sisters in the Imperial Building, where Fidel offered dinner for the demonstrators. The atmosphere was festive. In addition to the numerous Cubans, there were a few Peruvians, including Jorge Raygada. Talking with a group of Latin Americans was Marco Antonio Villamar, ex-congressman from Guatemala.

Fidel had prepared *spaghetti alle vongole,* which he later ate with us. Ernesto, sitting at my side, was silent. Fidel laughed and said: "Hey, Che! You're very quiet. Is it because your controller's here now?" Obviously, Fidel knew we were planning to get married, hence the joke. I then realized that they did a great deal of talking alone together. I knew very well that when Ernesto felt at ease he was talkative, he loved discussions. But when there were many people around he would remain withdrawn. Perhaps on this occasion he was a little more introverted than usual, because he was at my side and concentrating on taking care of me. Perhaps it was that we were celebrating a serious occasion—the forming of the 26th of July Movement.

Ernesto told me that they had agreed to publish Fidel's manifesto, that is, the defense speech he had made to the court in the Moncada trial, "History Will Absolve Me." This document would serve as the platform for the struggle, and so this meeting was historical. The 26th of July Movement was a brother movement to others already formed and fighting for the freedom and independence of their peoples, with a very important difference: Fidel Castro would dedicate himself to training a group of fighters that would sail to Cuba to fight against Batista's army, to defeat it and to make a true revolution for the people.

They told me about the ceremony, what a success it had been. There were several speeches, one by the Venezuelan Ildegar Pérez Segnini, whom I knew from Guatemala, followed by Raygada. The next was delivered by a Nicaraguan comrade, and lastly, Fidel's. His speech was magnificent, a real example of fine oratory in which he committed himself publicly to go and fight in Cuba.

It was also the night I met the Jiménez sisters, Eva and Graciela, both very good and charming women who helped Fidel a great deal, putting up several of the young men who were bound for the expeditionary force. They became sponsors of several of these men, buying them arms and equipment. Graciela, in particular, became a very close friend of mine; from that time on she was always invited to our parties, at which she used to sing revolutionary Mexican songs, accompanying herself on the guitar.

13

IN EARLY AUGUST I realized that I might be pregnant. When Ernesto came back from the hospital, I told him. He didn't believe it at first. "You're kidding," he said, but when I explained how I knew, he embraced me and kissed me.

"Now we should hurry up and get the legal ceremony over with; we also want to let our parents know. There's a doctor at the hospital who is also the mayor of a little town who will help us, and if he can't we'll go to the embassy. Tomorrow morning we'll go and take the blood tests."

We did as he said. He was already looking three months ahead, when I could take a test to determine the sex of the baby. The following afternoon he arrived with a present, a silver bracelet embedded with black stones, a fine work of Mexican craftsmanship. "This is for the baby," he murmured as he kissed me. Then he told me he had been paid in part for his work in the news agency, and so had thought of me. I wore this bracelet constantly as a good luck charm for our baby. I still have it, along with a dark red bathrobe that I gave him when we were married that he used to wear a lot.

We had almost decided to get married at the Argentine embassy. But at the last moment Ernesto enlisted the help of the doctor at the hospital who was also mayor of the beautiful little town of Tepotzotlán, where they agreed to marry us with only the medical certificate and our passports. We could have pretended that we were Mexicans, but we wanted to stay within the law and this was the most expedient solution.

Ernesto said either Raúl or Fidel Castro would be our witness. The date was set for August 18, exactly three months after we had gone to Cuernavaca, the day we considered to be the real wedding day, and the one Ernesto mentioned in his letter to my parents.

We went to Tepotzotlán with Lucila Velásquez, Raúl Castro, and Jesús Montané, the latter finally serving as official witness, since Raúl and Fidel wanted to avoid any involvement with the police. The legal ceremony was very simple but intimate and full of warm comradeship.

When we returned from the wedding Ernesto was very happy, and he prepared a roast for the group, which now included Fidel. Later, we told the news to all our friends; most of whom were exiles from Peru, Venezuela, and other Latin American countries, and some of them slightly resented not having been told in time for the wedding. We sent cables to our parents. My parents sent back a letter scolding us for not telling them in advance so they could have come for the wedding. They also sent us a bank draft for five hundred dollars as a present, asked us to send photographs, and Mother asked for a church wedding and said we should send her the exact date so that she could have the announcements made for our friends back home. They also sent me a power of attorney that I was to sign and mail to them, so they could protect my legal rights to the property that I owned along with my brother.

Ernesto answered the letter from my parents. I sat down at the typewriter and he dictated:

Dear Parents:
I can imagine your surprise at receiving our bombshell news, and can understand the flood of questions it must have provoked. You're of course correct in scolding us for not having informed you of our mar–

riage. We thought it wiser to do it this way, in view of the numerous difficulties that we encountered, not foreseeing that we would have a child so soon.

The pregnancy has been definitely confirmed; the biological signs along with the clinical data leave no doubt. Hilda is going through the pregnancy in perfect health and is very happy. Everything seems to indicate that there will be no major complications, just the standard conditions for a first birth.

We are very grateful for the expressions of affection you've given us. I know they're sincere: I've known Hilda long enough to feel that I know her family. I shall try to show that I deserve her at all times. I am also grateful for the "small gift." You've done more than enough. Don't worry about us. It is true that we're not wealthy, but Hilda and I earn enough to keep up a home properly.

I'm sorry to say that our political and religious convictions preclude anything but a civil ceremony. As for the date you wish to be included in the announcements, we leave it up to you. The real date is May 18. The names of my parents are Ernesto Guevara Lynch and Celia de la Serna de Guevara. On this point I must warn you that there is an absolute ideological barrier between me and my parents. I've made no formal announcement of the marriage (that is, no printed card), just written a letter like this to my parents and family friends about the marriage and the good news that they will soon be grandparents. It is very important for them because it's their first time; I'm the oldest, and only one of my brothers, just recently, is married. I forgot to mention that my parents live in Buenos Aires.

Hilda's power of attorney is a personal matter and concerns only her. The Mexican laws are different from yours and the only common property we have is the money we earn. We'll send pictures shortly. I am a rabid aficionado of photography and as such I couldn't commit the sacrilege of going to a professional photographer, but it happens that my camera—my loyal traveling companion—is sitting somewhere in the neighborhood of Tepico, where all stolen articles end up.

I believe this adequately answers your affectionate letter, but I should add something about our future plans. First we will wait for "Don Ernesto." (If it's not a boy, there's going to be trouble.) Then we'll consider a couple of firm propositions I have, one in Cuba, the other a fellowship in France, depending on Hilda's ability to travel *around. Our wandering life isn't over yet and before we definitely settle in Peru, a country that I admire in many ways, or in Argentina, we want to see a bit of Europe and two fascinating countries, India and China. I am particularly interested in New China because it reflects my own political ideals. I hope that soon, or if not soon someday, after knowing those and other really democratic countries, Hilda will think like me.*

Our married life probably won't be like yours. Hilda works eight hours a day and I, somewhat irregularly, around twelve. I'm in research, the toughest branch (and poorest paid). But our routines work harmoniously together and have turned our home into a free association between two equals. (Of course, Sra. Gadea, Hilda's kitchen is the worst aspect of the house—in terms of order, cleanliness, or food. And unfortunately, Doña Petrona [a well-known cookbook] *can't turn one into a good economist.)*

I'll let Hilda give you her own opinion about all this in a separate letter. I can only say that this is the way I've lived all my life, since my mother has the same weakness. So a sloppy house, mediocre food, and a salty mate, if she's a true companion, is all I want from life.

I hope to be welcomed into the family as a brother who has long been traveling the same path toward an equal destiny, or at least that my peculiarities of character (which are many) will be overlooked in view of the unqualified affection of Hilda for me, the same as I have for her.

With an abrazo *for the family from this new son and brother—*
ERNESTO

Practically everything he said to my parents in the letter was true, except, of course, what he said about my cooking. He was laughing as he dictated that paragraph to me. He put in the part about my writing separately to give me a chance to protest. But I couldn't make it clear to them that he was joking at that time because I had to deliver the letter immediately to a coworker who was traveling to Lima. I am, in fact, a good cook, especially with spicy Peruvian dishes that Ernesto could not eat because of his allergy. Like a good Argentine, he preferred a good steak and salad. There were, however, a few Peruvian dishes he liked that I prepared often for him.

It was also true what he told my parents regarding our travel plans. In late May or early June, Ernesto had brought up the possibility of going to work in Africa with the World Health Organization. After a while in Mexico we could go to some African country. To this end I arranged an interview for him with Dr. Samamé, a Peruvian and the director of the Pan American Health Organization in Mexico. Dr. Samamé received him very warmly. Dr. Samamé informed Ernesto that there might be a possibility for a fellowship in the field of parasitology for the following year. Ernesto told me that we should wait until I had been on the job for at least a year, to better my chances for a transfer in case he was granted the fellowship. We also wanted to visit Europe, and ever since our days in Guatemala we had been curious about China. I had also suggested India, whose beauty and charm had attracted me from childhood.

All these were plans for the next ten years, at the end of which we would go back to either Peru or Argentina. Our parents on both sides had offered homes and job possibilities in our respective countries.

But of course, all these plans and prospects changed forever with that conversation with Fidel.

14

DURING THE FIRST days of our marriage, Ernesto was very worried about a patient at the hospital whom he called "Old María." Very moved, he told me about her condition, an acute case of asthma. His interest was so strong that I almost felt jealous of that woman; she was on his mind all the time. Every morning he rushed to see her; when he came home the first thing he talked about was Old María's condition, and sometimes he would even visit her at night. One day he said very sadly that Old María might possibly die that night. He went to the hospital that evening to be at her bedside, doing everything possible to save her. The effort was in vain; that night the old woman died of asthmatic suffocation. She was very elderly and extremely poor; she had only one daughter and three or four grandchildren. She had been a washerwoman all her life, her years sad and hard. For Ernesto she was representative of the most forgotten and exploited class. His profound emotion was evident as he told me this, but not until later did I realize the mark the tragedy had left on him. When he departed on the *Granma,* I found a notebook of poems in the suitcase that he left with me. One of the poems was dedicated to Old María. It contained his promise to fight for a better world, for a better life for all the poor and exploited.

On weekends we generally went to the country; when we couldn't leave the city, we went to Chapultepec Park. We both enjoyed fields, trees, and the quiet of woods.

Sometimes in the evening we would go to the movies. Ernesto only liked funny pictures. We saw Cantinflas in *Arriba el Telón,* and I don't remember any movie that made him laugh as much. I laughed too, but mostly because he was laughing. A scene of Cantinflas dancing a minuet delighted him most. It reminded him, he said, of a school show in which they had made him dance a minuet. He was so clumsy it turned into a farce. Ernesto couldn't even follow music, much less dance.

We had moved from the house that we shared with Lucila to a small apartment of our own at 40 Nápoles Street, in Colonia Juárez. Fidel would soon be making a trip to the United States, and we planned a farewell dinner for him at our home, and invited Lucila.

I remember that Fidel came around a few days before the dinner. Ernesto was late arriving from the hospital that day, and we talked at length while waiting for him.

"What are your plans?" Fidel asked. "Ernesto says he's been paid for the news-agency work at the Pan American Games, so now you have a bit of money."

I told him we hadn't decided; we didn't know whether to buy an automobile or to take a trip.

"I think you should go on a trip," he advised. "Ernesto told me that you weren't able to go away after you got married. A trip would be best, but you could at least buy something for the house. Not an automobile—too many problems here in Mexico, papers and everything . . . if you need any help I have some friends who have an automobile. Better to buy something for the house, a record player or something like that."

He convinced me. We bought a record player, and in November we went on a trip to the Mayan ruins.

The night of the farewell party for Fidel, Jesús Montané and Melba Hernández arrived and stayed to eat with the rest of us. I had prepared a Peruvian dish and Lucila brought some Venezuelan food. Fidel congratulated us, commenting to Ernesto on how I had followed his advice and bought the record player.

Jokingly, Ernesto said, "She pays so much attention to you; I think it would be a good idea to take her along with us too."

Lucila was very interested in Fidel; we thought it might even come to something, because after he met her at our home, they had gone out together several times. However, he became so occupied with political problems that all other matters were put aside—or perhaps he had other girlfriends.

Suddenly Lucila asked me: "Tell me, Hilda, how did you snare Ernesto?"

Everyone laughed, and I could tell from Ernesto's look that he was going to come up with a mocking response.

"Well, it happened like this," he said. "I was going to be taken prisoner and she wouldn't tell where I was. She went to jail in my place, so out of gratitude I married her." The joke got another general laugh.

At another point in the memorable evening, someone asked Melba if she and Montané were going to marry soon. She said yes, and Montané nodded assent. Then Ernesto surprised me by asking gravely, "And who's *your* boyfriend?"

I looked at him, somewhat bemused. Then I understood that he was indirectly answering Lucila's earlier question. He had used the formal personal pronoun, *usted,* the form we used between us in arguments or when we discussed something very important.

"*Es usted,*" I answered. "It's you."

He came close and held me. "Of course it is. I'm your boyfriend forever. I have always been, and don't you forget it."

This I would remember later, when he was gone and I had only the notebook of poems.

Something else had happened that day that is worth mentioning. It had been agreed upon a few weeks before that I was to receive Fidel's mail, addressed to me under my maiden name. That day a letter came addressed to Señorita Hilda Gadea. Ernesto brought it into the kitchen, where I was cooking, and said, "Look, here's a letter for you." I told him to open it, and he said, "No, it's surely from one of your admirers."

"Well," I said, "it must be an *old* admirer, since he doesn't know that I'm married." We laughed and I opened the envelope, which contained a photograph. I glanced at the signature and it clearly wasn't for me. I put it back in the envelope and delivered it to Fidel that night at the party.

That evening was a happy one, with good talk and good music. We all wished Fidel success on his trip to the United States.

Later we found out that his trip had indeed been very profitable. The Cuban exiles in the U.S. received him enthusiastically; they were already organized in committees and able to offer him ample support for the revolution to overthrow the tyrant Batista.

SHORTLY AFTER WE were married a letter arrived from Peru—not for me but for Ernesto, and not from my parents. The return address read "Leper Hospital of San Pablo." I was curious; perhaps it was a job offer. When Ernesto came home, we were both surprised to find it came from the patients of the hospital who had been under his care. The letter was written in affectionate terms, congratulating him on his marriage and wishing him the best. Ernesto surmised that perhaps Alberto Granados had written them. The letter contained two photographs, a group portrait, and a picture of a football game.

"See how well they look," he said, handing me the pictures. I hesitated before taking them. He smiled ruefully, saying, "Don't be foolish. You have nothing to fear. You can't transmit leprosy by mail!"

I knew of course that it was a blood disease, but I guess it was the fact that I was going through the first months of pregnancy and instinctively safeguarding my child. The patients looked happy. Some of them didn't even look affected; others had the horrible marks of the disease on their faces, and still others were disfigured, the noses gone. Ernesto said that for many, the disease was arrested or practically cured, and that they were not contagious except through touching an open wound or continued close contact. I was moved by the thoughtfulness of the patients in writing him and by their gratitude toward someone who had come to them without prejudice. He was very happy to receive this letter; he answered it immediately and told his friends about it.

In September 1955 the headlines told of the imminent fall of Perón, of the ultimatum issued by the navy, of the people's demonstrations before the presidential palace. We pondered these turns of events, Ernesto expressing his hope that the people would fight to defend that popular government. I wanted it too, but unfortunately I saw certain signs that presaged a repetition of Guatemala's experience. We discussed it at length, sometimes heatedly; we spent those days waiting for news bulletins. My pessimism proved well founded by the ultimate outcome. Painfully we read of General Perón's resignation in order to avoid more bloodshed. The armed forces had collaborated with the Yankee oil interests to force his ouster, with the support of the big cattle ranchers and the Catholic Church.

The day the news broke Ernesto came home from the hospital early and stayed home that afternoon. He was distraught: "You were right, he has resigned. He has not fought. But the people *wanted* to fight. There was a mass demonstration in the Plaza de Mayo—they were machine-gunned."

Ernesto had appreciated the fact that the situation would be difficult in view of the many forces opposing the government, but up to the final moment he hoped that General Perón would enlist the people to fight against the enemy.

In the middle of this analysis someone knocked on the door, and Ernesto went to open it. It was the Peruvians, Raygada and Gonzalo Rose, a poet, along with the Puerto Rican Juan Juarbe y

Juarbe. "We're mourning the developments," was their greeting to Ernesto. We all felt the same: despair that the people weren't called upon to defend the government that had given the workers so much. For Ernesto the fall of Perón was a heavy blow; once again he was convinced that North American imperialists had intervened shamelessly in the affairs of our continent, and that one must fight this influence with the help of the people.

WE HAD TO wait until my vacation in the month of November to take our honeymoon. We had agreed to go south through the area of the ruins of the ancient Mayan civilization. We avoided planning an itinerary; we would take trains, buses, boats, or whatever without worrying about schedules, so that each day would bring its own surprises. Thus we would get better acquainted with the places we visited, see more and spend less money, and enjoy, simply and comfortably, a well-deserved vacation.

Traveling south, we came to the Papaloapán River. We talked about Bernal Díaz del Castillo's *Chronicles,* in which he tells of how the conquerors went through this area. In Palenque, we were intensely moved by the Mayan ruins, their majesty marvelously preserved through the centuries: colossal temples of distinctive architecture, the ball court, the stone sculptures of the gods, the famous Mayan steles—all those testimonies to the splendor of that civilization, one of the first on the American continent.

In Palenque I learned firsthand about the rigors of Ernesto's allergy condition. In Mexico City it wasn't noticeable. In fact I was surprised when I first arrived to find him so physically fit, as if he had never had asthma. He had even put on weight. Now, in Palenque, a tropical area, the asthma gradually intensified. It brought on our first spat of the trip, which didn't develop into a fight only because I stopped talking in time. Bothered by the asthma, he was taking antiasthmatic pills. It worried me, and I said, "Don't you want me to prepare an injection?"

He refused violently. I realized that he didn't want to feel protected, to be helped when he was sick. I kept quiet in the face of his brusqueness, but I was hurt. A while later, he apologized: "Forgive me. It's not your fault. This asthma drives me mad. Don't worry, this was a silly thing and not worth bothering over." Afterward he himself fixed and gave himself an injection, after which he felt better. The intensity of the attack subsided and we were able to move on the following day.

In Mérida we took a room in a small hotel, and from there we went by bus to Chichén Itzá and then to Uxmal. The visit to Chichén Itzá impressed us greatly. Ernesto, joyful, wanted to climb every temple. I gave out on the last one, the tallest. I stopped halfway up, partly because I was very tired, and partly because I was worrying about my pregnancy. He kept urging me not to be shy and to come on and join him. Actually, he too was afraid that the climb would be harmful for me and the baby, so he went on ahead, taking pictures of everything, including us. Tired and impatient from the heat, I ended up feeling and looking thoroughly cross.

I remember that a movie was being made in that area and there were many curious onlookers. Some small boys followed Ernesto, thinking he was an actor, and asked him for his autograph. He enjoyed the role. He didn't autograph their books, but he didn't correct their mistake, either. He just said, "I'm busy now," to our great amusement.

Uxmal was also very impressive, especially the stone figures, the friezes, the cornices, and the plan of its buildings. Ernesto was so enthusiastic that he intended, as soon as we got back to Mexico City, to buy a recent book about the Mayans we had heard about.

Next we went on to Veracruz, found a small hotel, and went out to see the city and the port. The only boat anchored in the Bay of Veracruz was an Argentine freighter, and it occurred to Ernesto to go aboard and ask the captain for some maté. We did and were

treated very kindly by the captain, who gave Ernesto several bag-
fuls. One can imagine Ernesto's joy. This find was a veritable treas-
ure for him. Maté of course was an inveterate habit with him; he
was never without his equipment, the *bombilla* (metal straw), *bo-
quilla* (mouthpiece), and a two-liter thermos for hot water. Studying, conversing, he always drank maté; it was the first thing he did
when he got up and the last thing he did before going to sleep. It
was almost a rite with him, and of course he had taught me how to
prepare it.

He found a fisherman's wharf and talked to someone about
going out on a boat. Arrangements were made. They went out at 2
a.m. and returned at 2 p.m. Ernesto was happy, enthusiastic over the
new experience. The only flaw had been a bad attack of asthma
from eating fish on the trip. He had to take an adrenalin injection
to get over it.

Later we went to another small fishing town. We spent some
time at the dock watching the fishermen at work and enjoying the
landscape. When we started back I had a sudden desire for fried
fish. Maybe it was one of those silly whims of pregnant women, or
maybe just the fact that I knew the fish would be fresh. Ernesto
suggested that we wait until we were back in Veracruz, where we
could eat more comfortably, but I really wanted to eat in this
place—I liked the simple atmosphere.

We went into a small restaurant, sat in a booth in the corner,
and ordered. There were some men at another table, apparently
sailors, drinking beer. One of them who seemed to be the head of
the group came over to toast with Ernesto, a Mexican custom.

"Well, then," the man said, "a toast to you, and another to the
Queen here."

Ernesto looked at him soberly and said: "Okay for me, but let's
leave her out of it."

I think these sailors thought I was a Mexican going around
with a gringo, because if they knew we were a married couple they

would never have made this breach of Latin manners. In any case the man went back to his table. After a while, when we had finished eating, he came back to offer another toast and insisted on "a toast for this Queen."

Ernesto's face got red. He got up, grabbed the fellow by the shirt with both hands, and, picking him up, carried him over to his table, where he dropped him in his chair. In a tough voice he said: "I told you, it's okay for me, but leave her out!"

For a few moments I thought something serious was going to happen. There were eight or nine of them and only the two of us. I began to think of what we could do. There was an empty beer bottle on the table; I could use it as a weapon if necessary . . . or one of the chairs. Fortunately, however, the proprietor intervened, warning them to stop bothering us or he would call the police. The police station happened to be nearby, but it wasn't necessary to call them because the men quieted down. I admired Ernesto's quick action and his refusal to put up with an offense. I was sorry I'd insisted on eating here. But it was one more opportunity, though unintended, to learn another facet of his character.

We visited Mocambo Beach nearby. We enjoyed the marked colonial flavor of the town. We felt at ease there. We took boat rides and many pictures. Ernesto observed that the area was still pure as far as Yankee influence went. I agreed; I told him about Acapulco—beautiful but completely Yankeefied by the tourist trade.

For the return trip to Mexico City, Ernesto proposed that we should start out on one of those small freighters that touch several points on the gulf. I was reluctant; the boat looked very frail, and it was also the hurricane season.

He teased me: "Are you afraid the boat will sink? At least we're both here. We'll die together."

"It isn't that. Maybe I'll be seasick—something could happen. I've never been on a long boat trip." I was afraid for the baby.

"Don't worry, nothing will happen. I'm here to take care of you," he said. He sounded so sure and confident that I gave in.

It took the small freighter three days instead of the scheduled one to arrive at its destination because we did get a hurricane. The sky was dark with huge, menacing clouds, and the enormous waves smashed the hull from both sides. The cargo broke loose, the boat listed dangerously, and they had to restow a lot of the cargo in the bow.

Almost all the passengers were seasick. I didn't exactly feel great either. But Ernesto was like a boy. Wearing swimming shorts, he was all over the decks, jumping from one side to the other, calculating the roll of the boat to keep his balance taking pictures and laughing at the discomfiture of the others. I was afraid something would happen to the baby. Ernesto made me stay in bed and drink only tea and lemon, and that's how I spent the whole trip.

The remainder of the journey we made by rail, motorboat, and finally by bus. (As we drew closer to the capital, I noticed that his asthma symptoms were less and less evident.) They had been fifteen unforgettable days of travel, with the immense satisfaction of being in each other's company at all times, alone in the midst of all that beauty.

BACK AT THE house we found a postcard from Ricardo Rojo. He explained that he had come through Mexico and had gone to Ernesto's bachelor apartment. There Patojo had told him of our marriage and had given him our address. The concierge had told him that we were traveling. We regretted having missed him.

15

December was approaching. The meetings among Ernesto, Fidel, Raúl, and the other Cubans were much more frequent, and so were their visits to our house. Ernesto advised that I be very careful with our other friends so that they wouldn't meet the Cubans. He also warned me that I should not be careless about any mail from the island or from the United States addressed to Hilda Gadea, because it was for Fidel.

There was to be a party on Christmas Eve, with a dinner prepared by Fidel and some of the other Cuban cooking enthusiasts, at the home of one of their friends. So on December 24, we met with the group. Fidel prepared the traditional Cuban dish, served on Christmas, called "Moors and Christians" (rice with black beans), roast pork, and cassava with garlic sauce. We also had the classic *turrones* (almond dessert), grapes, apples, and wine. Everything was exquisite. Melba Hernández and Jesús Montané were also with us. Melba was very surprised that I was eating everything, but I told her that the doctor was supervising my diet and that I could eat whatever I wanted.

That night Fidel held forth on projects that would be carried out in Cuba after the triumph of the revolution. He spoke with such certainty and ease that one had the feeling we were already in Cuba, carrying out the process of construction. That moment has

stuck in my memory ever since. He dwelled on the economic measures that would be carried out; he still trusted economist Felipe
Pazos and said something to the effect that "some very good ex-
perts will be helping *us*." He also spoke of the nationalization of
the main natural resources and principal sources of income. He had
Ernesto's complete support.

Suddenly, as if by design, there was silence. Fidel's last words
still echoed in my mind. I looked at Ernesto and he returned the
glance. In his eyes I could read the same thoughts that were going
through my mind. In order to carry out all these plans, it was first
necessary to get to Cuba. Fidel had spoken of invading the island
with a small force. This meant many difficulties, great efforts, and
sacrifices—all the dangers that must be undergone to achieve the
power for revolutionary change. I spoke first: "Yes, but first of all we
must get to Cuba."

"It is true," Fidel said gravely.

In each person's silence, one could almost physically feel the
thought and profound desire that Fidel's plans would material-
ize. Certainly all of us were thinking of the enormity of the task
and its inevitable toll of pain and death. For me the challenge was
terribly painful: to be separated from Ernesto and wait in a state
of agonized awareness of the constant dangers he would be forced
to meet. But I worried also about that marvelous group of true
comrades whom I already loved as if we had been together all our
lives: Fidel, Raúl, Juan Almeida, Universo Sánchez, Calixto García, Ñico López. It hurt to think of what could happen to them.
At the same time I felt proud of them and of what they were
about to do for the liberation of Cuba, the first stage in the liberation of our continent.

Ernesto confided that they would begin the actual preparations for the trip to Cuba in January. In August of the preceding
year they had begun periodic climbing trips to Ixtacihuatl and to
Popocatepetl, the two snow-peaked volcanoes near Mexico City.

Each man had his own climbing equipment. Ernesto invited me to go, but I had been waiting until another woman could go before taking him up on it. This woman was María Antonia, and Ernesto warned me: "You're going to meet a Cuban woman. She is a very respectable lady and a wonderful comrade, but don't be shocked by her fluent profanity; that's the way she is."

I bought all the necessary equipment, but it never came off. The Sunday we had decided on brought a storm with torrential rains, and we couldn't go. After that I was past the first two months of pregnancy and the strenuous exercise wouldn't have been prudent. But the rest continued going almost weekly. These expeditions were for the purpose of getting their muscles into shape; the preparation began in earnest in January 1956. I remember that Ernesto stopped eating steak for breakfast. At noon he had only a sandwich at the hospital, and at night he ate a light supper designed to keep his weight down; just meat, salad, and fruit, which was his favorite diet anyway.

Ernesto abandoned his allergy research program and turned down a professorship of a physiology course, which he had earned. From then on, upon finishing up at the hospital at about two o'clock in the afternoon, he went with the Cubans to a gymnasium to practice wrestling, basketball, karate, and judo. At first he came home stiff and sore, and it was my chore to give him a massage with special athlete's liniment. He said that later on they would go to a camp for survival training. Upon completing that training they would be ready for the boats, which Fidel was seeing about procuring.

During this phase Ernesto became interested in economics. I had some books by Adam Smith, Ricardo, Keynes, Hansen, and others on economic planning, investments, savings, devaluation, inflation, and other subjects. Each week he read a book, after which we exchanged our opinions on the subject. I was always surprised not only at the speed with which he read the books (admittedly

pretty dry reading) but also at the facility with which he grasped
their contents. Every night we discussed various economic topics.
He had been a book salesman at one time for a publishing house
that specialized in economics, and he was able to borrow several
books from them. In addition to these we read many other books
during this time, especially Soviet novels: *Thus Steel Is Forged, A
Man Complete*, and *The Defense of Stalingrad*, among others.

One day as he watched me touch-typing, he said: "Well, that
can't be so hard." I gave him a few basic instructions and he decided to learn to type. From then on he practiced for about a half
hour daily until he mastered it.

Ernesto liked tango music very much, although he could barely
tell one song from another. He admired the composer-singer Carlos Gardel and would have liked to play the guitar. One day he said,
"I'd give my right hand to be able to play the guitar." I burst out
laughing and replied, "Without your right hand you couldn't play
the guitar."

Since he couldn't follow the melodies of the various tangos, he
recited the words, always ending up with "The Day You Love Me,"
which he had recited to me ever since we had started going together in Guatemala. I had studied piano as a child and sometimes
I talked about the piano in my parents' house. One day he appeared
with a guitar, a present for me. He even asked Patojo to find someone who knew how to play. Patojo introduced us to a friend who
played for us, and afterward he came several times to give me les-
sons. But between my preoccupations and a lack of desire, I soon
gave it up. However, it was one of Ernesto's gestures that I most
fondly cherish.

Knowing my passion for classical music, Ernesto arrived one
day with three records for me: Beethoven's Fifth and Ninth Symphonies and Debussy's *Sea*. He immediately went to the record
player and put on the *Ninth Symphony*. He asked me to listen to it,
but I heard only a blare of jazz. "That's not the Ninth," I said. He

checked the record player and discovered that he'd forgotten to press the button and we were listening to a radio program. He made fun of himself for this, an additional piece of evidence that he lacked a musical ear.

Nevertheless, in time, he learned to appreciate classical music. During those months we enlarged our small collection of records. We bought selections of Beethoven, Schumann, Haydn, and Mozart. Ernesto liked to read with classical music playing in the background, and in time he could even distinguish between the *Fifth* and *Ninth Symphonies*. It was so great a triumph that I wrote his mother about it, who was pleasantly surprised by his progress.

ERNESTO HAD LONG ago removed himself from the photography venture, placing it all in the hands of Patojo. Our apartment had a small maid's room on the roof, which we let Patojo use as a darkroom. Cornelio Moyano, another Argentine friend from Ernesto's Córdoba days, had arrived from Argentina, and Ernesto happily helped him out by putting him in touch with Patojo.

We talked seriously one day about the fact that Ernesto's commitment to the invasion meant that we would have to give up our plans to go to Africa on the fellowship from the Pan American Health Office. Now we knew that *all* our previously planned projects would have to be abandoned.

Ernesto was aware of and accepted all the risks implied in the mission. We both knew the dangers that lay ahead; he himself had spoken about them, though he preferred to avoid such conversation because it disturbed me so much.

When I got emotional, he would say, "It is better not to think about it. We have to work and study more and more and keep those thoughts out of our heads." So we delved deeper into our studies on economics and our political discussions. We exchanged opinions. We alternated serious reading with light reading of novels and poems.

What remained very clear to me about the future was that he *was* going to participate in the Cuban expedition because it was part of the fight against Yankee imperialism and the first stage of the liberation of our continent. Afterward, the struggle would have to be continued in the other countries.

I was in perfect accord. I knew that I couldn't participate actively in the expedition because I was a woman and had to take care of the child I was expecting. But I could help by supporting the movement and carrying on propaganda activities.

According to our calculations the baby would be born sometime in March; the doctor said around the first week of that month. On the doctor's last visit, February 14, he said that the child would be born ahead of time, perhaps by the end of February. That day we moved to another apartment in the same building, located on the ground floor; it had more light and an extra room for the baby. I began having pains that night. I thought they might have been caused by the move, although Ernesto had done the heavy work. The pains lasted through the night, and in the morning Ernesto didn't go to the hospital; he went looking for my doctor. I went to the British hospital early in the afternoon.

Our baby girl was born that day, the 15th, at 7 p.m. Ernesto held my hand as I was taken into the delivery room; he said that he would be with me the entire time. We agreed that if the baby was a boy I would name him, but if it was a girl he would name her. He named the baby Hilda Beatriz, the second name given in memory of an aunt of his whom he loved dearly and with whom he had spent much time in his youth.

When they took me to my room, I asked Ernesto to see if I could have my baby with me. I was just coming out of the anesthesia and I still didn't know the sex of the baby. He told me that it was a little girl, but that he was very happy. A little while later, they brought her to me. It was overwhelming to have this new little being in my arms. She had an identification band with the name

Guevara. I studied her carefully; she really looked more like me. Ernesto was quiet, smiling serenely at the two of us.

Three days later he took me home. That same night Fidel came over, Hildita's first visitor. Fidel was enchanted with the baby, and as he held her he said: "This girl is going to be educated in Cuba." He said it with such conviction I was sure it would be so.

The next day, when Ernesto returned from his work at the hospital, he went right to the crib, enraptured. "This is what was needed in the house," he said to Hildita. He kissed her and rocked her in her cradle. It was truly a marvelous experience for both of us, and we were very happy.

The first night I didn't feed the baby. I had been told that if I didn't accustom her to being fed at night, she would quickly learn to sleep through the night. I had enough milk, but I followed instructions: it was important to get her on a schedule, since according to the law I had to return to work after forty days.

That first night she cried all night. In the morning Ernesto said, worriedly, "This afternoon we're going to take her to a pediatric allergist. You need to be given some advice, because the child cannot cry all night. If you have enough milk, I think you should feed her."

When he returned from the hospital, he had already made an appointment with the pediatrician. The doctor instructed me on how to care for the baby naturally and also told me what I should do to prevent her from developing an allergy. The first recommendation was to feed the child every three hours, even during the night. I could use powdered milk or formula as a supplement if I needed to.

It wasn't necessary. I nursed her on a strict schedule, and soon I was able to sleep almost all night. By the time Hildita was forty days old, she was sleeping through the night. When Hildita was ten or twelve days old, I developed a serious cold accompanied by high fever from inflamed tonsils. Ernesto immediately took over, staying home from the hospital, moving the baby to another room, and taking care of her himself. He brought her to me only to be fed, her little face covered with a cloth so that I wouldn't transfer my germs. He wasn't an advocate of antibiotics, but he gave me an injection to stop the throat infection and keep the baby from getting it. I mention all this to show the great concern Ernesto always had for the health of our child and the responsibility and tender care he always showed for both of us.

When I went back to work I had no major problems. I had permission to go to the house, which was close to the office, at feeding hours. I had a young girl helping me with cleaning and shopping and caring for the baby while I was at work. When I came back from work, the girl went to school. In my family it's always been a custom to encourage anyone working for us to improve themselves, and going to school was something Ernesto wholeheartedly approved.

On one occasion, I was on my way to the doctor's office and in the street I found a little kitten crying from hunger. It reminded me of my daughter and the idea of an abandoned baby touched me. I picked him up to take him home, but he cried and scratched so much I had to take a taxi and get home fast. It occurred to me that Ernesto might want to take him to the laboratory for allergy experiments. I didn't like that idea, but I wasn't going to make a big deal of it. Ernesto came home and I told him of how I had found the cat. Ernesto accepted him and gave him a name. When I expressed my relief that he was not going to use the cat in his experiments, he said, "No, this one's for the house." We trained it well and Ernesto grew very fond of him.

Since Ernesto had become involved in the expedition, he had withdrawn from many people and repeatedly asked me to be careful whom we entertained, to avoid security leaks. We saw only our most intimate friends: the Torres family, Doña Laura, Juan Juarbe y Juarbe, and Doña Laura's daughter, Rosita; and from time to time, the Guatemalan Marco Antonio Villamar, and Alfonso Bauer Paiz, and their wives; the sisters Eva and Graciela Jiménez; and the Cubans, Fidel and Raúl—constant visitors at our house—and Ñico López, Universo Sánchez, Juan Almeida, Calixto García, Octavio Rodríguez, and an unforgettable youth called El Guajiro. Patojo and Cornelio Moyano, the Argentine, were practically members of the family.

We frequently held intimate parties at our house or at the houses of some of the others, but almost always it was this same group. Ernesto didn't like large parties and refused to go to those connected with my office, although he never objected to my going. We did attend all political gatherings, for instance those of the Guatemalans as well as those of other Latin Americans. At small parties Ernesto would talk a great deal, mostly politics, and would go around offering maté to everyone. I remember the first time he offered maté to Fidel. He declined, first of all because it was bitter, and secondly because everyone drank from the same metal tube, which to Fidel seemed unhygienic. Ernesto laughed and kidded him, so finally Fidel drank a little. Later he became used to it.

Another time several Cubans came to dine with us, and Fidel brought a bottle of Cuban rum and cigars. Ernesto had already bought a bottle of mezcal, Mexican liquor fermented from cactus juice. Ernesto seldom drank, and on this occasion the mixture of mezcal, rum, and cigars—which he tried for the first time—left him a little dizzy, and he developed a headache.

Between my work, the house, and the chores imposed by the presence of the new baby, I had to cut out meetings with my Peruvian friends; I also did it for security reasons. Of the Peruvians, only Raygada and later the poet Gonzalo Rose came to see us. Ernesto liked Rose very much and they became very good friends. Rose would recite poetry, especially that of Vallejo, and occasionally some of his own. After the triumph of the revolution, around 1960 or 1961, Rose told me in Cuba that Ernesto had confided at that time that he was training to go and fight in a Latin American country. Rose had shown great interest and Ernesto made a date to introduce him to Fidel at a café. But when the time came, Rose was dubious; he thought it was going to be something inconsequential and didn't keep the date. Afterward, when the events of the invasion and the struggle in the Sierra Maestra became known, he regretted not having kept his appointment with Fidel and having missed the chance to become part of history with the eighty-two heroes of the *Granma*.

During this time we read Russian novels about the war against the Nazis. We also looked for anything having to do with wars for the liberation of a country; for example, China. We found very little, something of Mao and a few books on the popular armed movement in Latin America. One day Ernesto brought home *Storm in the Caribbean*, by Alberto Bayo, a high official in the Spanish Republican Army. Born in Cuba, Bayo had collaborated in Latin American attempts to launch an armed struggle. Comparing notes on his experiences, we concluded that perhaps guerrilla warfare was the way to power for the people in Latin America— but only by honest and dedicated groups, not by people like those Bayo described in his book. I never thought I would get to meet Bayo, but it happened when Ernesto was arrested, along with twenty of the future revolutionaries, in Chalco, a town near Mexico City.

16

THE PREPARATIONS FOR invasion intensified from April onward. In addition to the training they underwent in the afternoons, the men met in a kind of political circle to study Marxist works and discuss the problems of Cuba and Latin America in the evenings. Meanwhile, Fidel established contact with several Latin American political groups, especially the Guatemalans.

On weekends they not only climbed the nearby mountains but practiced target shooting as well. I remember that on one occasion Ernesto brought home a turkey, saying, "This is from Fidel." I don't know who shot it, but Fidel had decided that it should be brought to me. I cooked it—my first turkey—and prepared food to go with it. We invited a few of our friends and they all praised my cooking, which made me feel good. Ernesto kidded me: "This is a present from Fidel, and you have not saved him any!" I believe Fidel had been invited, but he couldn't make it that day.

Soon they would be going to train in the field, Ernesto told me, and perhaps they would leave from there. He couldn't tell me the date, but advised that I would find it out from the newspapers. The weekends thus occupied, we nevertheless got to spend time together some Saturdays and Sundays, and we would go to Chapultepec Park or to some little town nearby.

I remember one Saturday, before Hildita was born, when Ernesto was with the hospital doctors all day for some celebration or other. They had a football game, Ernesto playing on the side of the married doctors against the single doctors. Later they went to the house of Mexican ex-president Emilio Portes Gil, where Ernesto was put in charge of barbecuing a calf. He came home full of stories about a singer who had performed several tangos in honor of the Argentine doctor who had prepared the roast veal. The singer was Lucio Gatica, a Chilean who became famous later in Mexico.

Early the next day, Fidel and Montané came to take Ernesto away. I heard them talking about target practice, and I asked when they'd be back. "We don't know," was the answer.

"I could have lunch waiting for you," I said. "We don't know," again was the laconic response.

I was quite annoyed. They had upset my plans for Sunday, and since they weren't certain when they would return, I was going to have to stay home alone all day. Bored, I decided to go to the movies, to one of those neighborhood movie houses where they show two films and start early on Sundays. When I returned I found Ernesto, Fidel, and the other Cubans. Fidel had cooked roast pork and cassava with garlic sauce.

When I arrived they began to say their goodbyes, and I realized that Fidel was afraid I would say something. I was indeed upset, and I said to Ernesto: "What is this all about?"

He answered: "You go to the movies and we're stuck here alone, then it's you who is upset."

He explained that they had come back early, and that he had searched all over the house for a note saying where I was, which was our custom. When he didn't find it, he went out to call Doña Laura, thinking that I might have gone there, but she didn't know where I was. Fidel had then said: "I think you're going to have a fight, Che; it looks like Hilda is angry." Moreover, one of the Cubans, whom they called the Korean because he had fought there, had broken some dishes while washing them.

In the end everything came out all right. They had merely gone to look at some guns and then began to worry about me, so they came right back. We ended up laughing at our mutual irritability, and peace was restored.

It was in the latter half of May 1956 that they went off for field training, maybe to depart from there for the invasion, though Ernesto didn't know when. He said he would try to let me know.

A week after he had gone there were articles in the newspapers. Fidel Castro, and four companions, had been arrested because their immigration papers were not in order.

Now, I thought, trouble will come. I should be prepared for any contingency. I gathered up the correspondence I had received for Fidel. I went through all of our papers and took out anything political that could be used against us, including syntheses of books and notes that Ernesto had made on conducting a revolutionary government. I packaged it all together and took it over to Doña Laura. I told her in general terms what was happening. She was amazed: "Why wasn't I told anything?" I explained to her the necessity of tight security and added that I had gone to her only because I feared that the police might be coming to my house. "If anything happens," I told her, "I'll send you a message by Patojo."

Back at the apartment I found Patojo and Moyano; I told them what had happened. I said it was very possible that the others would also be taken, though I didn't know where they were, and that perhaps it would be better if they didn't come to our house so that they wouldn't be involved. They refused and said that, quite the contrary, they were going to come more often, to keep up on things and be able to help if necessary, since I was alone with the child. I was, in effect, alone, since the girl who helped me was still very young.

Patojo and Moyano left around eleven in the morning. A few minutes later, two men knocked on the door. One of them said, "Señorita Hilda Gadea?"

"No, Señora Guevara," I answered.

They insisted: "This is 40 Nápoles Street, apartment 5, and we are looking for a Señorita Hilda Gadea."

"I am Hilda Gadea Guevara," I said.

"Do you receive any mail?" they asked.

"Yes, from my family in Peru and Argentina."

"You got a telegram from another country," one stated.

"I don't know of any such telegram," I answered.

"Then you will come along with us to see the telegram, because it's compromising," they ordered.

"All right, but I'm taking my daughter. She's a four-month-old baby; I'm nursing her and can't leave her," I said.

They exchanged looks, and the one that seemed to be the boss said: "You don't have to come now—not yet—but don't go away. We will let you know."

When they left I thought about things. Two weeks had passed without any word from Ernesto. He usually sent word and asked for books or clean clothes. His last instructions had been to wait for word and he would tell me where to go to meet him. He was afraid the police might be watching the house. An hour had passed since the police left, and I decided to go out to the beauty parlor, to see if I was being watched. On my way back I met one of the group, Luis Crespo (he later sailed on the *Granma* and became a commander in the revolutionary army). What luck! He was on his way to my house to deliver a message. I explained the situation and warned him, "Don't go to the apartment. It's possible they might come back to take me. Go into hiding, and tell as many as you can what has happened."

I stayed in that afternoon. I figured there had been no observation in the morning, but there might be by afternoon. Around seven o'clock that evening, the same men returned and ordered me to go with them.

"With the baby?" I asked.

"Yes, with the baby," they answered.

I was taken to the federal police department in Plaza de la Revolución. There they showed me a telegram from Cuba saying that someone was coming to see Alejandro. "Alejandro" was Fidel's code name. Truthfully, I didn't understand the message. Everything that had arrived addressed to my maiden name I had turned over to Raúl and Fidel without opening. Emphatically I denied knowing anything about it.

"Who else lives in your house?" they asked.

"My husband, Dr. Ernesto Guevara," I answered.

"Where is he?" they asked.

"In Veracruz," I said, as Ernesto and I had agreed in case this complication arose.

"Where in Veracruz?"

"In a hotel, you can find out which one . . ." I replied. They then asked, "Have you two been in Veracruz before?"

"Yes," I answered, "on a holiday."

"What's he doing there now?"

"He's doing some research on allergy. That's his specialty. He works for the general hospital," I said.

Then they left me in an office. I waited and waited and finally protested: "I am a political exile. I want you to notify Senator Luis L. Rodríguez, who signed for my asylum, that I am here with my daughter. It is not very comfortable for the baby to be in a chair. I demand to be treated according to my rights. I want to see a lawyer and I'd like to know why I'm being detained."

They didn't answer. A while later they came back and one said, "We're going to have you meet someone face to face." They took me to another room where there were several detectives and a Cuban, they said. Indeed, his nationality was obvious as soon as he spoke. I don't remember his name, but I believe he was a doctor.

This gentleman admitted having sent the telegram to my house to set up an interview with the man named Alejandro, but he said he didn't know me. Nor did I know him, I stated, or anything about the telegram. Although I stuck firmly to my defense, the police continued to believe that I was hiding something from them, though they didn't know what.

They threatened to have me locked up. The first man came on menacingly while the second was gentle, but they repeated the same questions and tried to make me contradict myself.

"You're an intelligent and educated person. If you're not involved in anything, tell us where your husband is, who frequents your house, and anything else that would help establish your innocence. You must cooperate with us, and show your sincerity. . . . Tell us: do Central Americans come to your house?"

Dryly I replied: "No, only Peruvians."

"Are you involved in politics?" they asked.

"Yes, I am an Aprista. I am Hilda Gadea Acosta de Guevara. I was a student leader of the Aprista Party and it was the persecution in my country that made me come here," I replied.

"Do you belong to any political organization presently?"

"I am a member of the Committee of Aprista Exiles," I said, proceeding to give them the name of the secretary-general. They wrote down everything I said.

I persisted in asking for a lawyer. Then they told me they were going to question me some more. With the baby in my arms, I was taken to a dark room. As the door was opened, the light that filtered in from the corridor revealed a chair in which I was told to sit. I felt the presence of several people, but a bright light was shining in my eyes and I was unable to see anything in the room. I could see only blue spots; my eyes hurt.

A long and tormenting period of questioning began, intended to prove Communist infiltration of the Cuban group. Although I could not see, I had the impression that there was a North American present in the room, probably a CIA or FBI agent, since there would seem to be no other reason to keep the interrogators hidden. Unable to get what they were after, they decided to question me about specific facts. They asked me where and when I had met Ernesto. I told them that it was in Guatemala that we became engaged.

"Yes, we know about the relationship between you two. . . ."

"I don't know what kind of relationship you are insinuating. We were engaged," I retorted. They weren't really interested in our relationship but were after evidence of a Communist conspiracy.

Someone said, "Yes, Dr. Guevara has had relations with the Communists for quite a number of years."

"I don't know anything about that," I replied.

They went on about what we did, what activities, but it was all meant to establish the famous connection that threw them into a panic: Communist infiltration. They told me to confess that we had received money from someplace. I said we both worked. I had a good salary in the World Health Organization; Ernesto didn't make much money, but he worked at the general hospital. Again, they tried their best to make me contradict myself, but I was alert and said nothing incriminating, even to our friends. I repeated what I had told the other policemen, word for word, so there would be no discrepancy or pretext to keep me in jail.

Desperate because they hadn't discovered anything, they threatened to jail me for a long time. I insisted, almost aggressively, that they had to let me call a lawyer because I was a political exile.

Then they let me leave the room, and as I crossed the doorway I heard someone speaking in English, confirming my suspicion that there was a North American among them.

I continued to protest and demand a lawyer, and perhaps because of this they came around about 11 p.m. and said: "Lady, we're going to take you home to rest. You have to come back tomorrow to sign a statement."

The same two men who had arrested me took me home. I thought they would let me go, but no, they remained in the apartment. One of them asked: "Do you think your husband will come?"

"I don't know," I answered. "He usually comes on weekends, but he may not come today."

They hung around just the same. My mind was spinning.

What if he comes? How could I warn him? I just hoped that Crespo had been able to let him know. I was hoping for help from my friends, especially from Senator Rodríguez, because luckily I had been able to send a message to Doña Laura that I had been arrested. When the policemen came to pick me up, Patojo was in the little makeshift darkroom on the roof. It happened that, a short while before, he was entering the building with Moyano when they were stopped and asked where they were going. They replied that they were going to see Dr. Guevara. They were then asked who they were. They said that they were Mexicans. Moyano had been in the country only three months, and his Argentine accent was very pronounced. The police asked for his papers, which he didn't have with him. They took him to his apartment near the Ministry of the Interior, where, when he showed his Argentine passport, they arrested him. Since they had been taking pictures, the camera went with him to the jail—he never saw it again.

Patojo was luckier. His looks and speech backed him up, along with his student card from the University of Mexico. They let him go. He went up to his darkroom on the roof, from which he could communicate to our apartment by means of a bell.

Before going with the police that evening I had managed to ring the bell three times. It alerted him, and after we left, the faithful girl, Enedina, gave him a message to please inform Doña Laura so that she could tell Senator Rodríguez to help me. Patojo delivered the message, but when he returned, he too was arrested, and that night he and Moyano were locked up in the federal police headquarters, as were Fidel and four of his companions, María Antonia, the baby, and me.

When I returned home that night with the two policemen, I had the maid lock herself in the study while I locked myself in the bedroom. I could hardly sleep. I was nervous and jumped every time I heard a sound. I was sure Ernesto would come back and be arrested. The police settled themselves down on the sofa near the big window of the living room and stood guard all night to see if Ernesto came.

At seven o'clock in the morning, they knocked on my door and said that I had to go with them to sign the statement at police headquarters. I had no alternative so I went with them after they had declined my offer to have breakfast. I had only twenty pesos with me; all my money was in the bank. When we arrived at police headquarters, I discovered to my surprise that I wasn't there to sign anything but to be questioned again. I hadn't been able to eat anything due to my anxiety and I had to feed the baby, so I gave someone three pesos to bring me a quart of milk, the only food I consumed until noon.

The interrogation continued all through the morning. Two cops took turns; the one that pretended to be kind and mannerly and the brusque one who had threatened. I repeated exactly what I had said on the two previous occasions. They tried to convince me that I should save myself, that it was impossible for me to remain there with the baby, that I should tell them everything I knew, that they understood I was not guilty, that the guilty one was my husband, and that, if I didn't tell them all I knew about him, they could keep me in jail for many years.

Fidel knew I was there. He sent out for lunch for everyone who had been arrested, and he put me down on the list. But even more than the food he sent, the fact that my revolutionary brothers were near and remembered me made me feel good. It comforted and strengthened me during the difficult moments that I was going through: deprived of freedom, exposed to numerous threats, unable to contact a lawyer, without anyone to visit me, and with no comfort for the baby, who had to sleep in my arms all the time and couldn't be changed or bathed.

Around three in the afternoon they told me that I was going to go see someone, and I thought it was going to be another suspect. I prepared myself psychologically to deny that I even knew Fidel, if necessary. I entered an office, and there was Fidel with the police chief. Fidel got up and greeted me very affectionately. I was going to pretend I didn't know him, but he insisted on showing his concern, "This is not possible, Hilda. I can't allow you to be here with the baby. Please tell them that you did receive letters for me—being a political exile, I had no permanent address and had asked you to receive mail for me, addressed to you."

I couldn't refuse Fidel, but I thought he was being forced to say this, so I tried to stall. "Only if you have spoken with Ernesto," I said.

"No," he said firmly. "We are involved in more important things. You make this statement so that you'll be freed, because I can't let you and the baby go through these discomforts and dangers."

When he insisted a third time, I gave in. I signed a statement in accordance with Fidel's instruction and with the approval of the police chief. Then I asked the chief about my two friends arrested the night before, Cornelio Moyano and Julio Roberto Cáceres (Patojo). He promised that they would be freed and he kept his word; Moyano and Patojo took me home. I noticed a change of attitude on the part of the police; they were attentive, particularly the chief, who treated Fidel with deference and with whom Fidel spoke easily. It seemed as though everything was arranged. Afterward Patojo explained the reason for the change in treatment: apparently Lázaro Cárdenas, the former president of Mexico, had intervened.

The others were at a ranch somewhere outside the city, and I was happy thinking they would be safe. Unfortunately, for security reasons, I didn't know where the ranch was located, or else I would have sent Patojo to warn them. Luckily no one had mentioned that there were some comrades at a ranch, because I didn't think the police would leave it at that. But Patojo had discovered something while he was locked up.

"I think Fidel has been forced to say where the ranch is," he told me. "At first when we were all together in the same cell, the other Cubans didn't trust me, but Fidel explained that I was a friend of Ernesto, and from then on we were one group. At one point after his interview with the police chief, Fidel called them together to show some pictures of the ranch. I think he arranged something with him. I think Fidel has had to agree to take the police up to that place to avoid a gunfight. I heard that he will go in first and the police will follow."

17

WE SOON GOT the answer. The next morning a newspaper story said that a group of twenty or twenty-one people had been arrested, among them an Argentine doctor, Ernesto Guevara. The article speculated that this was an international plot, because among the Cubans were a Peruvian Aprista exile and a Communist Argentine doctor. In addition to the group captured at the ranch, the newspaper said that Fidel, María Antonia, and four other Cubans had been arrested in the city. The information was vague and sensational and it didn't say where they were being held. It was my duty to find them and I was joined by the other Cubans in the effort.

I went to the Argentine embassy because the commercial attaché was a distant relative of Ernesto's family. We were supposed to visit him but had never gotten around to it. I explained to him who I was and why I had come to see him. He was very cordial, possibly because he was related to us, but quite taken aback—how was it possible that an Argentine was mixed up in this when he should be in his own country? I told him that we thought differently, but this was certainly not the moment to discuss how we looked at things or the problems of the peoples in our continent. The matter at hand was the imprisonment of an Argentine citizen who might be ill-treated and suffer hunger and humiliation. My bluntness made an impact on the diplomat and the embassy made inquiries. They advised me that Ernesto was being held at the Immigration Detention Center on Miguel Schultz Street, as the

Cubans had already discovered on their own. I went there immediately with clean clothes and food. The first week I wasn't allowed
to see Ernesto. Thereafter I could see him on Thursdays and Sundays, but I brought food for him and the others daily. The Cubans
did the same for another group.

One day while I was waiting at the door of the detention center to get in to see Ernesto, I later learned from Patojo, several men
came to our house saying that they were the police. I assumed it
was federal police until I discovered that they had taken personal
letters from Argentina, along with the replies that Ernesto had
written and I was going to mail. It couldn't have been the federal
police, because they've already done this once, I thought to myself.
Which police could they be? Who would be interested in searching our house to find out about us? There was no doubt: it had to
have been Batista agents.

When I was able to talk with Ernesto, I told him about it but
he dismissed it. "You're always oversuspicious," he said. But later
Fidel said: "Hilda's right, of course; this is the work of Batista's
agents. The police here had no reason to make another search."

The first time I was able to visit Ernesto I asked him immediately how they came to be discovered. He told me the police already knew where they were. Possibly they had learned of their
whereabouts from Batista agents, who were constantly trying to
follow them. The police even had pictures—the ones they showed
Fidel—and they were ready to take the ranch by force. They accepted Fidel's terms that he would take them to the ranch in
Chalco and go in ahead of them, to avoid useless bloodshed. The
fight, after all, was in Cuba, not in Mexico.

Ernesto also told me that he almost escaped. When they came
he was up in a tree on guard duty. He saw the approach of the military jeeps, and even when he saw Fidel get out, he knew something was wrong. But he was forced to come down when a
comrade said that Fidel wanted everyone. But only those who were

there at the time were captured; another group, which was out with Raúl, was saved. They were behind a nearby hill where they stored the arms.[1]

When they took him to be questioned, he was the only one handcuffed, and once, as they were pressing him to explain his international ties, they threatened him: "We have your wife and your daughter in jail, and if you don't talk we're going to torture them."

He decided he would answer no more questions. "If you want to beat me, go ahead," he told them. "Since you're so savage as to jail a woman with an infant, nobody can expect justice from you. Up to now I have answered your questions; from now on, I won't." And he didn't, infuriating the police, and bringing harsher treatment on himself.

All the questions they asked Ernesto were aimed at finding an international link; that is, that foreign Communist governments had sent him to infiltrate the Cuban group. When I told him about my questioning in the dark interrogation room and about the English-speaking man, we knew that the CIA or FBI (it made no difference which) was seriously worried about the possibility of Communist influence in the Cubans' activity. This, of course, was entirely untrue.

Mexico City's newspapers played up speculation on the group's capture. Our Latin American friends were very nervous because of the intense police scrutiny and persecution. Nobody came to our house except those intimate friends I've mentioned. The newspaper *Excelsior* published a letter from the secretary-general of the

---

1. At the ranch Ernesto had gotten me a dog, a white crossbreed. I liked dogs and had talked to Ernesto about my Dachshund back home in Peru. But when he was arrested he had to leave the dog at the ranch of course. It was as if I had received it, though, knowing that he was thinking about me.

Aprista Party in Exile, in which he denied any responsibility and assured the government that the local Peruvians respected Mexico's laws, that they hadn't done anything untoward, and had nothing to do with the Cubans. This hurt Fidel very much and he had Ernesto tell me, "Look what your Peruvian comrades are doing!"

In truth I was ashamed. I had never expected such a lack of solidarity from my comrades. It was their position but not mine.

There was, on the other hand, a good attitude on the part of the Guatemalans. Alfonso Bauer Paiz went to see Ernesto in spite of the risk (one had to one's give name and address before being allowed to see the prisoners), as did Ulises Petit de Murat. Paiz's visit was interesting. He saw things as a lawyer and thought that filing a separate appeal for Ernesto as an Argentine would work. Fortunately he talked to me before he talked to Ernesto, and I suggested that it would be better to consult Fidel first; I was sure that Ernesto wouldn't accept. We did so, and Fidel approved, but when we explained the idea to Ernesto, he said: "By no means! I want the same treatment as the Cubans." I had expected this reaction, but felt that it was my duty to clarify the alternatives open to him, since it was the suggestion of a well-intentioned friend.

On one of my first visits to the prison Ernesto gave me the first draft of a poem he had written while at the ranch and asked me to keep it. There were a few additions scratched in here and there. The title was "Canto a Fidel"—a song to Fidel, and it was a poetic pledge that they would fight beside him in Cuba, to victory or death.

But at the moment, imprisoned as they were, the possibility of bringing this to reality seemed remote. I asked him if Fidel had read it.

"No," he said. "Now's not the time. I wrote it to give to him after we sail."

I had this poem published in Lima, while they were still fighting. Unfortunately the printer lost the original, but later on I was able to take copies of it to Cuba.

One time when I visited Ernesto in jail, he pointed to a slender young man: "Do you remember him?"

I looked at him; he reminded me of someone but I didn't recognize him.

"It's Chuchu," he said.

It was indeed "Chuchu"—Jesús Rodríguez—who would later serve as one of the navigators of the *Granma*. I could hardly recognize him. He had been somewhat chubby with a round pink face; now he was pale and had lost more than forty pounds. I asked him what had happened. "Nothing," he said with a laugh. "Except that they wanted me to make a statement, so they beat me twice a day, put me in a tub of cold water, and gave me nothing to eat. This went on for a week. They wanted me to tell them where the arms were."

Knowing the answer, I asked whether he had said anything. "Of course I didn't," he said. "I don't know anything."

During my visits Ernesto and I talked about the rough, almost savage procedures of the police in our respective countries. We figured that they were being encouraged to do this by the FBI. Analyzing the situation of our own group, Ernesto said: "There is no doubt that the FBI is mixed up in this, to defend Batista. He represents for them the control of the sugar industry and commerce. The Mexicans can't be that interested in hunting down the Cuban revolutionaries. Not only that, they have made their own revolution and they know what it is to take up arms. It's those Yankee *hijos de las chingadas,* sons of bitches, as they say here."

Another thing: the special police assigned to this case took all of Ernesto's and the Cubans' belongings—clothes, watches, books, etc. We lost our second typewriter, which was never returned to us, despite our claims. Ernesto was left with what he was wearing and a few sport shirts and slacks. His only full suit—Ernesto never had many clothes—was also confiscated. Universo Sánchez, realizing that Ernesto had practically nothing to wear, asked for his size so that he could get him a suit. (This happened after most of the Cubans had been set free and only Ernesto and a few others remained in jail.) I told Universo that I was sure Ernesto wouldn't accept, but I was surprised to discover that he did. Universo got him a beige suit—which Ernesto promptly gave to Calixto García, who was in the same predicament as far as clothes went. Later, when Ernesto came out, we took money from our family budget to buy him a dark brown suit, a color he preferred.

While Ernesto remained in prison, I brought him cooked food, but after a while he told me that he preferred to receive raw meat, raw vegetables, and fruits so that he could cook his own meals as the Cubans did. One Thursday he told me firmly: "Starting tomorrow, don't bring me anything more. We're going on a hunger strike to force them into a decision."

I thought it was too much, but who was I to say anything? I myself had gone on a hunger strike in Guatemala. Ernesto knew what was going through my mind, and was waiting for me to say something. I understood, then, that if I objected it could be interpreted as a selfish concern with my own worry over him. I said nothing.

He smiled and said calmly, "Nothing is going to happen, two or three days or even a week without eating doesn't kill anyone."

The next day, when I went to visit them, I found to my surprise that Fidel's terms had been accepted by the authorities and that he and eighteen others had been released. Now only Ernesto and Calixto García were left; their immigration papers weren't in order. The threat of a hunger strike had had positive results, and if they weren't all free it was because of purely legal questions. For those who remained, the treatment improved.

Ernesto asked Fidel to go on with his plans as scheduled and not to change them on his account. But Fidel said that he would wait and that furthermore he would do everything possible to free them. As usual, in all his decisions, Fidel was being fair, but if events had forced an earlier departure without Ernesto, would the course of the Cuban Revolution have changed? I sincerely think that it wouldn't have. Ernesto, however, wouldn't have found the opportunity to emerge as a revolutionary leader.

That same night, Fidel came to our home with a doctor, Faustino Pérez. This man would be one of the twelve *Granma* expeditionaries who held out in the Sierra Maestra. He became a *comandante* in the force and later president of the Hydraulic Resources Institute.

Fidel didn't remember our apartment number and shouted from below: "Hilda . . . Hilda!" I answered him and they came up. He patted the baby a while and then said, "Don't worry, Hilda; we're free, but we're doing everything possible to get Ernesto and Calixto out. Try to arrange asylum for him, if possible in El Salvador, so he can go there by car with Alberto Bayo, who is married to a Salvadorean, and then come back in another car. But don't worry."

The next morning I went immediately to try and obtain the asylum. The Salvadorean ambassadors agreed in principle but said they had to get ratification from their capital. Meanwhile there were encouraging signs. Fidel said that we would still have to wait a bit, but he hinted at a private deal and a sum of money that might persuade the authorities to set Ernesto and Calixto free.

In all they were in prison almost two months, during which I visited every Thursday and Sunday. One of my fondest memories is of Ernesto playing with our daughter during those visits. We met in a large patio where prisoners could play football to keep in shape. There I would spread out a blanket and put Hildita under an umbrella. Ernesto played for long periods of time with Hildita until she fell asleep, then he would watch her, observing every gesture the baby made in her sleep. At other times he would pick her up and carry her proudly around the patio. He loved his daughter very much.

Of the original group of prisoners, those I knew personally in addition to my husband and Fidel were: Universo Sánchez, Calixto García, Juan Almeida, Jimmy Hirtzel, Arturo Chomón, Ciro Redondo, Aguedo Aguilar, Cándido González, Julio Díaz, Oscar Rodríquez, Reynaldo Benítez, Santana Bondechea, Alberto Bayo Jr., Horacio Rodríguez, Raúl Vega, and María Antonia González.

The regular visitors of this group were: Señora Carmen del Bayo, General Bayo's wife and Alberto's mother; Alberto's wife, also named Carmen; Armando Bayo and his wife, Selina; Gabriela Ortiz; Lidia Castro, Fidel's sister; Raúl; Eva and Graciela Jiménez; and Carlos Franqui.

It was in these none too agreeable circumstances that I first met Señora Carmen del Bayo. General Bayo was military training adviser to the *Granma* fighters. After the success of the revolution he would be made commander of the Cuban Revolutionary Army, the highest rank. Bayo was born in Camagüey to a Spanish father, and he grew up in Europe, where he became a pilot in the Spanish air force. In 1936 he and his group took the islands of Formentera, Cabrera, and Ibiza, and landed in Majorca. On September 4 he directed the withdrawal of troops and weapons from Majorca. From 1937 to 1939 he was military aide to the minister of war. That year, after losing an eye, he went to Mexico, where he took a post as a professor in the air force cadet school in Guadalajara. In 1948 the Nicaraguan revolutionaries gave him the rank of general and engaged him as technical adviser to the guerrillas. He published several books about his experiences, and in 1955, Fidel Castro asked him to take charge of the training of future expeditionaries.

Señora Carmen told me that General Bayo had wanted to turn himself in if the police would let the group go. He had sent a letter to the newspapers to this effect. It went unanswered by the police when it was published, and, in agreement with Fidel, he had decided not to surrender himself.

(Bayo told me that during those days he had to remain in hiding at a health spa, where he met a *gringa* who was staying at the same hotel. Going for a swim, she handed him the key to the safe-deposit box where she kept her jewelry, and Bayo left it in his name at the desk. When they finished swimming, his new friend asked him for the key and he hurried to the desk to get it. Incredibly, however, he couldn't remember the false name under which he had registered. The minutes dragged by while the clerk looked at him coldly. He made superhuman efforts to remember, but to no avail. Finally, in desperation, he was about to blurt out some story or other when the name suddenly came to him: Manuel Mangada.)

While they were all there together in the Schultz jail, the farewells after each visit were beautiful. Prisoners and visitors gathered around together, and we would sing the Cuban national anthem and the hymn of the 26th of July. The prisoners joined arms to make a solid barrier symbolic of the vanguard of the people. We were all moved; all of it—prison, the fraternal feeling, our common ideals—had a deeper meaning for us. It was more than simply that our loved ones were suffering in prison; it also meant the knowledge that the task and the efforts would continue until Cuba was liberated. There was a communal confidence that all difficulties would be overcome. It made these moments unforgettable.

Whenever I have been present at one of the great parades and large gatherings in Cuba after the triumph of the revolution, I have always seen in my mind those farewells in the Schultz jail, as if no time had passed. It was then that my faith was renewed that a strong, well-led vanguard will carry the people's struggle to victory.

I can perceive in all its dimensions what Fidel always meant, from the conception of the movement throughout the incredible campaign: preparation, the *Granma* expedition, the invasion. Fidel was always the unifying element of all those patriots, true representatives of the people, who sincerely wanted to change the structure of the exploitive society of Cuba. They were all willing to risk their lives to succeed, and they all trusted Fidel absolutely. He guided them like an older brother, with love but with strict discipline. It was no naïve enthusiasm they brought to the task. On the contrary, among the expeditionaries, including Fidel and Raúl, I always saw a deep understanding that the enterprise would be hard, very hard, and that it meant risking their lives. But with this they had an indestructible faith that they would attain their goals.

They were such a marvelous group, full of the joy of life, but a life that had to mean something positive for humanity, with such a complete purity of purpose that one had to respect them and be confident they would succeed.

Ernesto had total trust in Fidel from the beginning. Knowing how profound, disciplined, and severe he was in judging himself and others, I could thus appreciate Fidel's stature. Besides this, on my own I was completely convinced of Fidel's importance and of the great role that he would play in Cuban and Latin American history. From the first time I met him, his formidable personality was evident, as well as his vision and understanding of the problems of our continent; a vision on which he and Ernesto agreed totally.

18

THE IMPRISONMENT HAD lasted about two months when I rushed home from the office one afternoon to pick up some things to take to the jail. I went hurriedly toward the baby's room to see how she was doing. Suddenly I saw a shadow behind the door. I went in, and there was Ernesto!

We hugged each other joyfully and stayed that way for several minutes, after looking down at the crib where Hildita slept peacefully. He was delighted by my surprise in seeing him: "I didn't want to call you at the office; I decided to surprise you here. Besides, I was dying to see love's petal most profound."

After explaining that he and Calixto had been set free because Fidel had given a large sum of money to the authorities to arrange all the immigration matters, he talked about how surprised he was by the baby's progress: she hadn't cried all afternoon and she had grown so much. Hildita was four months old when Ernesto was first arrested, and now she had just completed her sixth month. I said she was a good baby because of her schedule: her tranquility proved it was just right for her.

He told me he could spend only a short time at home, and then he had to go finish his training. They had decided to split up into very small groups and live incognito in small towns until their departure. He thought that it would be delayed since there were many details to take care of, but this time it was necessary that they remain underground in their activities.

He applied himself to arranging his papers, answering his mail, piled up by now, and writing to his family in Buenos Aires. Hildita, who spent most of the time in her playpen, observing everything while she held onto the bars of the crib with her chubby little hands, was beginning to mouth syllables. Ernesto felt badly about having forgotten what the baby's voice sounded like, and he would sit next to the crib talking to her or reciting poetry. Sometimes the two of them would burst out laughing.

He was home for three days. On the fourth he got his things together and said goodbye, promising to keep in touch with me. A week later he sent a note through Comrade Aldama. The note instructed me to go with the baby to Cuautla and gave me the name of a hotel in that town, where I should ask for Señor González. Friday was a holiday, so we could spend three days together, since I did not work on Saturdays.

The baby suffered from a slight cold, but I decided to take her because I knew what it would mean for Ernesto to see her. We arrived at the hotel, I asked for Señor González, and then came an unforeseen dilemma.

"Which Señor González?" the hotelkeeper asked. "There are two."

I didn't know what to say. I hesitated, finally deciding on Ernesto González. At that moment Ernesto appeared. This was, in fact, the name he had used. He was very happy to see us. He rocked the baby in his arms and caressed her. Then he became quite concerned about the cold—her first—and said that I shouldn't have brought her, the first consideration should have been his daughter's health. I calmed him down: after all it wasn't that serious, and I hadn't wanted to deprive him of the pleasure of seeing her. The next day she was back to normal.

I told Ernesto that Aldama had delivered his money—everyone in training received a small sum for basic expenses—and that I had brought it with me. He asked me what money I had used to get to Cuautla. I laughed and assured him that it was money from my salary. He was so honest and conscientious about the money that came from the movement. Collected through great effort, these sums had to serve only the most essential needs—transportation, housing, food, and the like—never for personal family matters.

Since May, when the preparations intensified, Ernesto had been gone from the hospital and had no income. My salary had to pay for all the household expenses. This was nothing remarkable, of course; we were not only husband and wife, but also comrades, participants and supporters of the 26th of July Movement. It was a principle not to touch a penny of what he received, especially because I was working.

Field training in the small towns of Mexico lasted about two months. By November they had reason to believe that the precautions they took had caused the police to lose track of them and they became more confident. The traveling wasn't good for Ernesto because it often took him to tropical areas, sometimes close to the ocean, thus aggravating his asthma. That's why he began to come home weekends.

During the week someone always came with a note from Ernesto, asking for books or sending me letters to be mailed. I would send back his mail by these messengers. I still have one of the notes, brought by El Guajiro. It reads:

> *Hilda:*
> *The bearer is a dumb* guajiro [*peasant*]. *Don't waste time on him.*
> *Just show him the baby so he'll appreciate the quality of the bull. A*
> *big hug and a little kiss, from—*
>   *CHE.*

The note included a message for Moyano, asking for a number of books on Marxism that Ernesto wanted him to get at the library. It ended with the following: "Get them as quickly as possible. Be sure they are there when I get there Saturday."

One note said that he couldn't come home that weekend, so I accepted an invitation from a coworker to accompany her to the concert of a famous Soviet cellist. As I was getting ready that Sunday, Ernesto arrived. I explained about the date and said I would phone my friend and tell her that I wouldn't be going. He insisted that I go as I had planned. When I got back, he ragged me about abandoning him for music. Actually, he had enjoyed the three hours I was away playing with the baby, reading, and drinking maté. He decided to stay until Monday, explaining: "I have to make up for the hours you spent at the concert, leaving me alone."

At the ranch, before the prison period, Ernesto had developed a great admiration for Bayo, "the Old Man," as he was affectionately called. He told me how the author of *Storm in the Caribbean*, wanting to be an expeditionary, had gone on a crash diet to lose excess weight. He had lost twenty-two pounds in fifteen days and he wanted to lose ten more by following an even stricter diet, but there wasn't time. Ernesto ended by saying: "What a great old man!" I was surprised, since few people impressed him so strongly. He added, "He's a great chess player. We had some memorable games when we finished working. At first the Old Man didn't want to admit that I could beat him. He plays very well—really the only good adversary I've had in a long time."

Ernesto was amused by the Cubans' mania for cleanliness. When the daily work was done, they all took baths and changed their clothes. "That's fine," he said, "but what will they do in the hills? I doubt we'll ever be able to take a bath or change clothes. The most we do is save enough soap to wash plates and eating utensils so we won't get sick."

During the underground period, when Ernesto came home, he used to like to take care of the baby while I was busy cooking or busy with household chores, as our young girl helper went home on Sundays. Hildita was about eight months old at the time and she was no problem. She amused herself when she wasn't sleeping by playing by herself in her playpen or walking around it by holding onto the railing. When Ernesto tired of reading, he would take her in his arms and recite poetry to her, loud enough so that I could also hear. Sometimes when he stopped reciting, the baby would cry, and stop only when he started reciting again. Every recitation always included Machado's poem "Listen."

Taking Hildita in his arms one day, he looked at her tenderly and said: "My dear daughter, my little Mao, you don't know what a difficult world you're going to have to live in. When you grow up, this whole continent, and maybe the whole world, will be fighting against the great enemy, Yankee imperialism. You too will have to fight. I may not be here anymore, but the struggle will enflame the continent." He spoke very seriously. I was overwhelmed by his words and went to him and embraced him.

He called Hildita "my little Mao" because of her somewhat slanted eyes. In this she resembled me. He would say she was Chinese like her mother, although my slanted eyes come from an Indian grandmother. At the same time, of course, he was implying his admiration of Mao Tse-tung.

During these weekends at home we continued to exchange ideas and discuss books on economics, particularly Keynes's work *The General Theory of Employment, Interest, and Money*. He also practiced his touch-typing, which he could handle surprisingly well considering the lack of practicing time. In the countryside he had no typewriter, and the only chance he had to use one was when he came home on weekends, so I had borrowed one for him.

On one of those weekend evenings he recited a poem that he had composed for Hildita: "To Hilda Beatriz in Adolescence." His mood surprised me because we usually didn't talk about the future. Sometimes when I got sad he would say, "Cheer up. Just keep working and don't think about it. . . ." That night, however, he was moved as seldom before, when he read the poem. Then he gave me the original. It was a beautiful poem, which said, in essence, that he was wandering without direction through the paths of America, that he had stopped in Guatemala to learn about a revolution, and that it was there that he found a comrade who had been the support and inspiration of his ideals. The two of them had defended a small country attacked by Yankee imperialism, and later, in Mexico, he had decided to go and fight for another small country, a piece of our continent, to defeat exploitation and poverty and help build a better world for Hildita, "love's petal most profound." At the end of the poem, he explained metaphorically the reasons why he was going to fight, and hoped that Hildita too would fight for justice, not only for her country, but for her whole continent.

Unfortunately this poem, too, was lost in Lima during the time the terrible news of the landing came out, and my billfold was stolen along with the other poem from when he first proposed in Guatemala. In those later days his letters were few and far between; the news reports were vague, and I carried those poems as talismans that would keep him alive—not from superstition, but because of the great love that they bore, and the fervor of hope that he would succeed in the hard revolutionary trial.

One weekend he brought some notes on emergency care of the wounded. He had made a summary of the first-aid medical data, and I typed up several copies. He explained that although he would go as a doctor on the expedition, he would also be fighting, and that it was crucial to teach others first-aid techniques in order to care for the wounded who could not be brought to hospitals.

Every time he returned to the interior, it could have been farewell, because he couldn't tell me ahead of time when they were going to leave. This uncertainty, the repeated agony, brought us closer together. Trying to cheer me up once, he said that perhaps we would have a little free time to go to Acapulco. He would let me know the hotel where he was registered, and I could join him there with the baby for a farewell celebration.

One day, we were arranging books on the shelves, and almost casually Ernesto stopped and took me in his arms. He stroked my hair and looked at me with a tenderness that I had never seen before, and said gravely: "It is possible that I might be killed, but the revolution will succeed. Don't ever doubt it. We are prepared for all eventualities."

I held him tightly while he kissed my hair.

I had begun to be hopeful about the Acapulco trip, even if it was only for a weekend. Then came the news, from the newspapers as well as from some comrades, that the police had broken into the house of a Cuban woman in Lomas de Chapultepec, where Pedro Miret was staying, and that they had confiscated some weapons and arrested him. On Saturday, when Ernesto came, I told him about it. He reacted calmly, saying only that precautions had to be doubled because the police might be watching. Early Sunday, El Guajiro came. I knew right away he was nervous from the way in which he asked, "Where's Che?" I told him that Ernesto was taking a bath, whereupon he marched right into the bathroom. When Ernesto came out, still combing his hair, he said calmly: "It seems that the police are on the hunt, so we have to be cautious. We're going to the interior and I probably won't be back next weekend. Sorry, but we'll have to leave our Acapulco trip until later."

I became upset. I had the feeling something was going on.

"Is something going to happen?" I asked.

"No, just precautions," he answered, gathering his things and not looking at me. When he finished, he went to the crib and caressed Hildita, as he always did before leaving, then he turned, held me, and kissed me. Without knowing why, I trembled and drew closer to him.

Later, I would always remember how he tried to remain natural at that time, and I knew how much he must have forced himself. He left that weekend and did not come back.

19

HE HAD BEEN gone a little over a week when Alfonso Bauer Paiz called me at the office and asked me to come to his house. When I arrived he told me that Ernesto and Calixto García had been in his house for a few days, and that when Ernesto left, he had asked him to wait a week and then call me to get his suitcase and other personal belongings. He gave me several books, a suitcase, and some clothes that didn't fit into the suitcase. Among other things inside the suitcase, I found a notebook with his poems.

Bauer Paiz told me about those last days that Ernesto stayed in his house. An apartment in the same building was robbed one day, and the police came to investigate. They began questioning everyone and searching all the apartments and servants' rooms. Bauer Paiz had no time to let his guests know; Ernesto and Calixto locked themselves up in a servant's room.

Ernesto had heard the unusual sounds and been alerted. So when the police knocked on the door, he quickly covered Calixto with a blanket and then opened the door. The police looked inside and asked who was sleeping in the bed. Ernesto said it was a friend who was sick. The police left, unsuspicious.

Ernesto had to do that because Calixto's dark coloring might have attracted the attention of the police. If they had questioned him, his accent would have betrayed his Cuban nationality. This would undoubtedly have brought on complications, which had to be avoided at any cost on the eve of departure.

The next morning, they left without saying where they were going. I knew then that they had gone to Veracruz, to begin their trip to Cuba.

Not all of those who had prepared for the invasion were able to go on the expedition. Not only was a traitor detected among them, but Fidel was only able to get one boat. Characteristically, Fidel managed the departure right under the noses of the police. As we found out later, they left from Tuxpan, in the state of Veracruz, on the yacht *Granma*, whose normal capacity was twenty, but on this trip she accommodated eighty-two. This was the last week in November 1956, and I knew absolutely nothing at the time, although I anxiously scanned the newspapers every day.

As Ernesto and I had agreed, I left the apartment as discreetly as possible, taking things out gradually, and went to live with Doña Laura. We had told her earlier that Ernesto would be going into the interior to carry out some allergy research, and that I would stay in her house while he was gone. Doña Laura asked no questions and took me in with her usual affection, like a daughter.

Our plan was that I would wait until I knew definitely of the invasion from the newspapers. I would then go with the baby to Peru to await the outcome. If they were successful, Hildita and I would join Ernesto in Cuba. We would stay for a while and then decide whether to go to Peru or Argentina to continue the fight. It was Ernesto's definite intention to continue fighting in other countries of Latin America: "My intervention in Cuba is only the beginning of the Latin American struggle," he told me. I agreed and always encouraged him to go on.

He had left a letter in the suitcase to be mailed to his parents in Argentina, and a note to me with reassurances that I would soon get news and not to worry. Up to the last moment he tried to comfort both his parents and me, knowing the pain we would suffer because he was in danger, though he knew he had my support. I would have liked to be with him.

After the departure of the *Granma*, I met some of the Cubans who had not been able to go on the expedition at General Bayo's house. They told me that Fidel had been forced to choose on the basis of weight, and that some of them, such as the Aldama brothers, had been left out because they were too big. These comrades said that many of those who could not be included cried at not being able to risk their lives for the freedom of their country. They also told me that "Che"—they all called him that now—was a man of great courage and great sacrificial spirit. They described with admiration how Ernesto, in training people to give injections, had them experiment on his own body. He would get up at five o'clock in the morning and share the chores like everyone else. Then later he would perform his own special tasks as chief of personnel, and in addition he would take water and food to Raúl's group, which was situated farther away behind the hill. One of them said to me: "Che may not be a Cuban, but he is our true brother."

I subscribed to the newspapers *Excelsior* and *Novedades* in order to get them at home early and be able to go through them before going to the office. On December 2 the papers were late, and I left the house without a chance to read the news. When I arrived at work I found everyone looking solemn. There was an embarrassed silence, and I wondered what was happening. Then I became conscious that everyone was looking at me. A coworker handed me a newspaper and said: "We are very sorry about the news." I read the headlines: "INVASION OF CUBA BY BOAT—Fidel Castro, Ernesto Guevara, Raúl Castro, and all other members of expedition dead . . ."

I could not go on reading. My head began to spin and I had to sit down to keep from falling. In a flash the whole thing went through my mind, from the time we had met in Guatemala until that last Sunday when I saw him leave. It was one thing to be in favor of the expedition, and another to face the pain of loss. Now it was time for the pain.

The head of the office came to me and said: "Don't work today. Go home and rest."

I hardly had the strength to get a taxi. When I arrived home Doña Laura had already read the news. She embraced me, saying: "I'm sorry. No one told me . . ."

"Forgive us, Doña Laura, but we couldn't say anything."

"I understand," she said. "I suspected it would be something like this, but I didn't think it would be so soon."

She left me to rest. I locked myself in my room. I didn't want to see or speak with anyone. After a while Doña Laura came back. "I don't want to insist," she said. "I know what this news must mean to you, but I only want to tell you that in these cases one must wait for confirmation. Because many times—it's happened to me—the report turns out to be false. I know words won't help much; I know what you're going through. But keep in mind my own experience."

She went on to tell me of some events that had to do with her husband, Don Pedro Albizu Campos. Sometimes, she concluded, the police find it convenient to spread false rumors as a tactic to discourage people from supporting a cause.

I thanked her. Her explanation comforted me, and that afternoon when General Bayo arrived I was able to listen to him calmly. He didn't believe that they were dead. With conviction and faith he said to me, "Hilda, I can tell you this: he's the most intelligent, the cleverest—the one who profited most by my instruction. I'm sure nothing has happened to him. We'll find out, Hilda." There was so much assurance in his words that I calmed down a lot and was even, after a while, able to eat something. Thereafter I was always in someone's company—the general or a member of his family, Myrna Torres, or Rosita Albizu stayed with me while we waited for confirmation.

Ernesto's father called me on the phone. He had called his cousin who was the Argentine ambassador in Cuba. The cousin reported that Ernesto was not dead, nor among the wounded or prisoners. This still wasn't certain news, but it was something. Then at my office they told me that the doctor who was a representative of the Pan American Health Organization had said the same thing. The hope that Ernesto was alive was strengthened considerably. I lived on that hope.

I continued working toward getting out of the country. In order to avoid contact with government agencies, Ernesto hadn't left the necessary paternal permission for me to leave with the baby. He hadn't gone to the foreign relations ministry but had instead written a simple paper that I was to take to a notary public. But the announcement of his alleged death meant the Mexican government would hardly accept this. I went to the Argentine embassy and had Ernesto's signature in the note notarized, and thus was able to get Hildita's exit permission. I arranged for my vacation from the office, and planned on going to my parents in Lima. The last few days in Mexico I was so upset and worried by the lack of news clarifying Ernesto's situation that I was unable to take care of our belongings. I gave most things away or just abandoned them.

On December 17 I left for Lima with Hilda Beatriz, then ten months old. I traveled by plane with a stopover in Guatemala City. During the time we were at the Guatemalan airport, the police watched me closely. I didn't dare even call some of our friends for fear of compromising them.

My family was very happy to see us. I had been away for a few years and they had never seen the baby. My mother was very worried about Ernesto's fate, while my father expressed pride that his son-in-law was involved in such a movement. He agreed with our ideals and thus felt somehow personally involved in that revolution.

Ernesto's family invited me to Argentina, and I agreed to go after spending a month with my family. Toward the end of December, Ernesto's father telephoned to tell me that he was mailing my ticket, and we agreed that I would leave after January 6.

Then he gave me the great news: "I've just received a note from Chancho. . . ." My heart jumped; "Chancho" was Ernesto's Córdoba nickname. The note read, "I have spent two lives, I have five left.[1] Trust that God be Argentine."

Ernesto was alive!

Joyfully we departed for Buenos Aires.

ERNESTO'S PARENTS AND his brother and sisters, Anna María, Celia, and Patatín (Juan Martín), were waiting for me at the airport. Later at the house, his other brother, Roberto, and his wife came to see me. They all were attentive from the beginning, making me feel at home, and displaying unending affection for Hildita, of course. Ernesto's parents were quite happy to have us there.

This was truly a nice household. Ernesto was certainly the favorite son in the home, an attitude shared by all members of the family, especially the aunts, who still referred to him as "Ernestito."

His parents' first question was why Ernesto had decided to take part in such a movement instead of coming back to Argentina to work. The second was: "Who is Fidel Castro?" I explained at length what Ernesto and I thought of Fidel, and what he had done in 1953 during the Moncada attack; I told them of the deep faith and trust that workers and students had in him, and of the conviction of the best Cubans that this was a necessary road to a new life, no matter what sacrifices were demanded.

Because of their deep affection for Ernesto, his parents found it hard to adjust to the idea of his being in danger. They kept coming back to the feeling that it would be better if he were in Argentina. I explained to them nothing would deter Ernesto, considering his views on life and Latin American problems. In an-

---

1. A reference to a cat's seven lives—as the Latin American expression puts it.

swer to their question of how he had arrived at these ideals, I said there were many factors that had converged to form him into what he was. One of these was the criminal intervention of imperialism in Guatemala, which he had seen firsthand and which had impressed him to the point of resolving to actively fight imperialism from then on.

I told Doña Celia, my mother-in-law, of the deep tenderness that Ernesto felt for her. This was no an exaggeration for her sake: I knew what she meant to him. She suffered continually, with the agonizing question apparent in all she did: "Where is my son?"

One evening after supper they showed me the family album. One by one I looked at pictures of Ernesto, from childhood on. There was one that particularly caught my attention; although Ernesto had the look of an adolescent, he was very small and still wearing short pants. His mother explained that this was common in the family; the Guevaras didn't begin to fill out until after age fifteen.

That day Ernesto's mother had been especially anguished over the absence of news after that first note, in which, incidentally, they had positively recognized his handwriting. His mother's worry had had a strong effect on me, as had the photos; I slept very badly that night, dreaming about him, dressed as he was in Mexico, coming to my room with a smile on his face and telling me that he was all right.

The next morning I told my mother-in-law that I thought Ernesto was all right, because of my dream. I don't believe in dreams, but I wanted to cheer her up. Around noon the mail arrived, with a letter from a cousin in the United States who had been visited by a comrade from the 26th of July Movement. The letter brought definite news—Ernesto was fine; he had been wounded in the neck but had already recovered.

It was a fiesta day for everyone. Don Ernesto declared with emotion that if Ernesto were captured in Cuba, he would go there in a boat and rescue him!

Then someone in Mexico wrote, confirming the cousin's story: the radio report said that Ernesto, after having been wounded in the neck, had disappeared in a field of sugar cane, that the Batista soldiers had set fire to the field and that nothing further was known. Now his mother and I were terribly worried again: Ernesto, wounded in the neck, with asthma, in all that smoke. We didn't know how serious the wound was, whether he could even talk. We knew what had happened, but not knowing all the facts was torture.

Ernesto's parents took very good care of me. They took me to visit the aunts and other members of the family, all of whom were very kind to Hildita and me. One day my in-laws asked me if I would prefer to stay in Buenos Aires, where it was quite hot, or go to the country, to a small house they had in Portela. The point of my trip was simply to be with them and to wait with them for news from Ernesto, but if there was a chance to be in the countryside I thought this would give us more privacy. So we left Buenos Aires, where the temperature in that 1957 summer heat wave reached more than 110 degrees. It was also quite hot in Portela; we spent most of the day in bathing suits near the swimming pool. Hildita was in the water so much that she caught a bad cold and had to take penicillin shots for the first time in her short life.

Don Ernesto had remained in Buenos Aires and every two or three days came to Portela to see us. The whole family had become so fond of Hildita that they asked me to let them christen the baby; Don Ernesto and Celia, the sister, would be the godparents. I didn't believe in the rite, and I knew that Ernesto didn't like it either, and, really, neither did the family: they only wanted to be closer to Hildita. However, I agreed to do it, provided they explained to Ernesto that it was their idea.

So the month passed in Argentina, amid the affection of Ernesto's family, as we all awaited news of Ernesto—news that never arrived. The baby and I went on to Peru.

20

AT THE AIRPORT in Lima, one of my sisters greeted me joyfully: "Ernesto wrote to you!"

"How do you know?"

"Because we opened it," she said.

I protested: "But it was a letter for me!"

"But we were just as anxious as you." She went on, "The envelope had Cuban stamps and we were sure that it was from him. We opened it but the handwriting was illegible, but it does say something like 'Ernesto . . .'"

As soon as I arrived at the house I read the letter. At last I was hearing from him. He was alive, and he was thinking of me and the baby. He expressed his deep trust in the campaign that had begun and in the future of our struggle. I remembered his words of farewell in Mexico: "Anything can happen to us, but the revolution will triumph."

Knowing what it would mean to them, I wrote his parents and forwarded Ernesto's letter, asking them to please return it. From then on, although always with a certain anxiety, we looked forward to his letters. This is what the first one said:

January 28, 1957
My dear old lady,
Here in the Cuban jungle, alive and bloodthirsty, I'm writing these inflamed, Martí-inspired lines. As if I really were a soldier (I'm dirty

and ragged, at least), I am writing this letter over a tin plate with a gun at my side and something new, a cigar in my mouth. It was rough. As you probably know, after seven days of being packed like sardines in the now famous Granma, *we landed at a dense, rotting mango jungle through the pilots' error. Our misfortunes continued until finally we were surprised in the also now famous Alegría and scattered like pigeons. I was wounded in the neck, and I'm still alive only due to my cat's lives—a machine-gun bullet hit a cartridge case in my chest pocket, and the bullet ricocheted and nicked my neck. For a few days I walked through those hills thinking I was seriously wounded because the bullet had banged my chest so hard. Of the boys you met there in Mexico, only Jimmy Hirtzel was killed, executed after surrendering. Our group, including Almeida and Ramirito, whom you know, spent seven days of hunger and terrible thirst until we were able to slip through the cordon and, with help from the peasants, get back to rejoin Fidel. (One of those reported possibly dead is poor Ñico.) After lots of difficulties we got reorganized and rearmed and attacked a troop barracks, killing five soldiers, wounding others, and taking some prisoners. It was a major surprise to the army, which thought we were completely dispersed. They increased martial law rules throughout the country and extended them for 45 days more, and sent troops after us. We fought them off and this time it cost the army three dead and two wounded. They left the dead on the mountain. Soon after we caught three guards and took their guns. Add to all this the fact that we had no losses and the mountain is ours and you'll get an idea of the demoralization of the army. We slip through their hands like soap just when they think they have us trapped. Naturally the fight isn't all won, there'll be many more battles. But so far it's going our way, and each time it will do so more.*

Now, to you. Are you still at the address I'm writing to? And how are you all, especially "love's petal most profound"? Give her the biggest hug and kiss she can take. To the rest, an abrazo *and my best. With my rushed departure I left my things at Pancho's. Your pictures and the baby's are among them. Please send them when you write. You can write to my uncle's house, using Patojo's name. The letters will be delayed a while, but I think I'll get them. A big* abrazo *for you.*

    CHANCHO.

Along with everything else, during those days, I had the misfortune of losing my mother. The emotional load broke me down physically and I had to see a doctor. He recommended that I try to keep my mind occupied, busying myself with a variety of tasks. I began to work as an auditor in a school and I kept the accounting books for several small businesses. In addition, with the idea of carrying on propaganda for the 26th of July Movement—or M–26, as it was now abbreviated—I rejoined the Aprista Party. Soon I was elected to the post of secretary of statistics on the National Executive Committee.

From the moment I got Ernesto's first letter, I searched for some way to help the M–26. The struggle was very difficult and the odds great. But Ernesto still had enthusiasm and faith in the success of the venture, if each worked in whatever area he could. I couldn't fight in Cuba because I had to take care of my daughter, but I could carry out tasks outside.

I asked General Bayo, with whom I regularly corresponded, to put me in touch with the Committee for Activities Abroad. He did so, sending the address of José Garcerán, who was in charge of the Mexican committee. Later he would be smuggled into Cuba and would take part in the action against the Goycuría Barracks, where he died. Garcerán put me in touch with the New York committee, headed at the time by Mario Llerena, and he, in turn, sent me a credential so that I could represent the 26th of July Movement in Peru. Afterward the committee would be headed by Antonio Buch, Haydée Santamaria, and José Llanuse; Llanuse was in the office when final victory carne.

I worked, complying with the instructions sent to me by the committee, on propaganda and money collection. The committee would send me the newspaper *Sierra Maestra*, Fidel's speeches, and the news bulletins that were issued in Sierra. I would have these reprinted, distributed, or published in certain newspapers and magazines in Peru. I founded a movement for the liberation of Cuba, with the support of the members of the leftist wing within APRA, and we were able to help several Cuban exiles who took refuge in Peru.

Letters came from time to time from Ernesto. Only a few of mine managed to reach him, although I followed his instructions. He never got the pictures of the baby and me he had asked for. Later, when I had set up formal communications with the committee in New York, he began getting my letters. When Hildita was two years old, on February 15, 1958, I wrote Ernesto and asked him to authorize my coming to the mountains of Cuba, to be with him and help; the child was then old enough to be cared for by either my family or his. His reply took about four or five months to arrive. He said I couldn't come yet; the fight was at a dangerous stage, and an offensive would begin in which he himself wouldn't remain in any one place. The coup of March 13 by the Directorio against Batista had failed, as had the strike of April 8 sponsored by the 26th of July Movement, and the opposition was intense. But in the mountains Fidel and his comrades grew stronger daily. Not only had they turned back the June–July offensive of Batista's army, but they had opened a second front, commanded by Raúl Castro. They planned to come down from the mountains onto the plains in August.

Several more times there were announcements of Ernesto's death in combat, each a time of anguish for me. I particularly remember toward the end of December 1958, the news that Ernesto had died in the battle for Santa Clara, heading the column Ciro Redondo. This was the battle that had been fought by the people of Las Villas province against the Batista puppets, in which the people derailed the bulletproof train carrying government reinforcements. With this action, government resistance was practically wiped out. On January 1, 1959, the bloody ex-sergeant Batista fled the country with his closest collaborators.

The well-known events that followed now belong to history.

It was also on January 1, 1959, that I arrived in Havana with my little daughter. With the candor that always characterized him, Ernesto told me forthrightly that he had another woman, whom he had met in the campaign of Santa Clara. My pain was deep, but, following our convictions, we agreed on a divorce.

I am still affected by the memory of the moment when, realizing my hurt, he said, "Better I had died in combat."

For an instant I looked at him without saying anything. Though I was losing so much at that time, I thought of the fact that there were so many more important tasks to be done, for which he was so vital: he *had* to have remained alive. He had to build a new society. He had to work hard to help Cuba avoid the errors of Guatemala; he had to give his whole effort to the struggle for the liberation of America. No, I was happy that he hadn't died in combat, sincerely happy, and I tried to explain it to him, ending with: "Because of all this, I want you always."

Moved, he said: "If that's how it is, then it's all right . . . friends, and comrades?"

"Yes," I said.

The divorce was granted on May 22, 1959. Ernesto remarried on June 2.

21

THE TWENTY-FIVE MONTHS of struggle in the sierra, months of hunger and privation, and insufficient sleep worsened Ernesto's allergies and brought on frequent severe attacks of asthma. During the final stage of the campaign in the mountains of Las Villas, he developed a minor tubercular condition in one lung. Nevertheless, he continued to work intensely.

It was the first days of the revolution, with a whole society to be changed. There were visitors from all over the world, especially Latin Americans, who wanted to see Fidel and Che. Ernesto received people into the small hours of the night. The doctors advised that he try to cut down on work, and for this reason he was moved to a small chalet on Tarara Beach near Havana that had been confiscated from a Batista supporter. But visitors continued to flock in, and he received people until dawn even while bedridden.

Sometimes he sent for Hildita. During the entire time he was really ill he wouldn't let her enter his room, nor would he kiss her; he would watch her from a distance. After his tubercular condition cleared up, he moved to an old house in Santiago de las Vegas. She would visit him there also, two or three times a week, whenever he sent for her. When he was all right and could approach her, I sent Hildita along with some photos that had been taken in Guatemala and Mexico to cheer him up. Hildita told me that he had been very happy looking at the pictures, and she said: "We had a good time." He asked to get copies made, and, telling me this, Hildita asked:

"Mommy, am I from Guatemala too?" I told her that she was entirely from Mexico, but she went on with how enthusiastic her father had been over Guatemala, and how he would never forget that part of his life. Neither would I.

During one of the first television interviews, a newspaperman asked him: "How were you treated in Guatemala, Commander Guevara?" "I was persecuted, my wife was put in prison and thrown out of the country by way of the Mexican border," he replied.

I was watching it at the time, and I was touched that he should remember me like this. I wasn't yet his wife in Guatemala, as he had stated, but I wish I had been; it would have meant one more year by his side.

IN 1959, I was working on the Farm Housing Commission, an organization that built homes for the farmers whose houses had been devastated by fires and bombing by the Batista army. We worked in the National Institute for Agrarian Reform building, where Ernesto was working on the eighth floor. He was director of the Department of Industrialization, which later became the Ministry of Industry. Our daughter was now three years old, and from time to time I would take her to see her father, leaving her off on the eighth floor, and returning to my office on the fourth floor.

One day, around the latter part of October, I went to pick her up and, as I was leaving, Camilo Cienfuegos arrived to see Ernesto. Camilo was charming, with an all-embracing smile. He knelt before Hildita and kissed and hugged her. He picked her up, and, seeing that the child was curious, prompted her to pull his beautiful beard.

"Does it hurt?" asked Hildita.

"No, because I am very strong," he replied as he laughed and winked.

"How is it that you have such a long beard?" she asked. "Because every day I pull on it a little," he said. "Look, like this!" Hildita laughed and, convinced, also pulled his beard. That is the last remembrance I have of Camilo. A few days later he disappeared on a plane, on his way to Camagüey to handle the outbreaks that occurred as a result of the agrarian reform program.

Two days earlier, I had heard Cienfuegos' magnificent speech before the government palace. During the first days of the revolution's power, the expeditionaries of the *Granma* who had been killed were brought to Havana and buried. I was present at the funeral, and on that occasion Ernesto introduced Camilo to me. Ernesto asked him if he remembered me from Mexico, but I don't think we ever met there. However, Ernesto had spoken about me during the trip and in the mountains. Another time Camilo came into my office unannounced while Ernesto was in Egypt. He sat down, took off his wide-rimmed hat, and rested his head in his hands, remaining in silence for some time. Afterward he excused himself, saying, "I am very tired." He asked how Hildita and I were. When he left, he was wearing his happy smile again. I realized that he was concerned about us during Ernesto's absence and the visit served to calm him down.

THE BAY OF PIGS battle lasted three days. We were very worried about Ernesto; a rumor circulated that he had been the victim of an assassination attempt and that he was wounded. But within a few hours a soldier came by the house with a message from him, telling us not to worry. His own gun had accidentally gone off and he had suffered a slight wound. But he gave no further details. When the battle was over and the revolutionary forces had won, he came to the house to see Hildita and told us about the fighting. The gun had fallen from its holster and gone off, the bullet grazing his cheek. "It was an unimportant accident," he said as I looked at the face wound, "but it was another close call. An inch closer and I wouldn't be here to tell of it," he finished casually.

I continued to correspond with his parents after our divorce. Don Ernesto wrote me in 1961 that he wanted to return to Cuba to see his grandchildren and that he was saving money for the trip. One day when Ernesto came by the house, I suggested that he bring his father to Cuba. He answered impatiently, "So you're one of those who don't believe I'm on a fixed salary, and can use the public funds as I like."

I was surprised, and finally answered, "I didn't mean that, I only suggested that you pay your father's passage since your father wants to come. You can pay it back on installments."

The fact is that I hadn't thought of all the implications; I explained to him that it was just that I was thinking the trip could be made fairly cheaply by sea. He calmed down and said, "All right, but let's leave it for later on. Now's not the time."

I was sure that the revolutionary government would have invited his parents immediately, and as many times as he wished. But I also knew it was Ernesto himself who imposed the restrictions, and I knew they meant a great sacrifice for him: one of the traits that made me believe in him from the first was precisely his deep love for his family.

Ernesto worked very hard in the different posts the revolution assigned him. First he was director of the Department of Industrialization at the National Institute for Agrarian Reform, then president of the National Bank, and finally Minister of Industries, always working under the self-discipline he applied daily to himself ever since I first met him. He kept up with his work, he received many visitors, and he still found time to study and learn, writing a bit every day. During the years he remained in Cuba he would stay up until dawn, working. He was always punctual for his appointments, and he spent weekends working in the fields or in the factories.

But he didn't like the bureaucratic life. He considered it his obligation to the revolution to remain at his post: a new society had to be built. Such obligations, however, were trying for him. He often commented about this. Once when he was visiting Hildita, taking her in his arms, he said: "When, oh when, my darling daughter, am I going to find time to get away from all this office work and spend a couple of weeks with you in the country—just the two of us?" And he added to me: "One of these days I'm going to take Hildita to the country, maybe to Oriente. Have everything ready."

He never made it. Several times he almost succeeded, but at the last minute obligations always came up.

IT IS ANOTHER part of history now—those days when U.S. spy planes discovered the existence of missile sites in Cuba. Fully justified, Cuba had petitioned the Soviet Union for them, to defend herself against a possible attack by the Yankees, an imminent danger that still hadn't passed.

The incident produced anxious moments all over the world, but especially in the United States, over the imminent possibility of a nuclear war. Cuba was doing nothing more than using all the means possible to defend herself against surprise attack. The memory of the frustrated Bay of Pigs invasion of 1961 and the defeat of imperialism were fresh in the minds of the Cubans. As a worker, I witnessed the calm but firm reaction of the Cuban people in the defense of their land and their revolution during those days of October 1962. I was full of admiration for Cuban courage during those difficult times when an atomic attack was expected any moment, a courage that still had time for light spirits and a sense of humor. It would be impossible to recount the innumerable anecdotes of those days. The dismantling of the missile sites, the negotiations, and Cuba's admirable reactions are also part of history now.

As the point of danger passed, the lady who took care of Hildita called me at work one day and nervously said: "Come home right away, the commander is here." I went home and found Ernesto, in dirty uniform and muddy boots, with Hildita, happily playing with the dog. The babysitter told me, crying, that when he got there he asked immediately for the child and me. He went to

Hildita's room, picked her up, and carried her to the living room. They both sat down on the floor to avoid dirtying the chairs. Ernesto then kissed Hildita and said, tenderly: "Dear little daughter, I hardly ever get a chance to see you. We have been through great danger on account of those damn Yankees. When you grow up you'll know all about it. I had to come first to see you." There were general tears from the babysitter, the neighbors who had come in, and even the soldiers with him. There were comments: "How he loves that child—he had to come right here first."

Ernesto and I talked for a while. It was good to see him playing with the baby. I didn't want to pester him with questions. It was enough to see him alive and know that this time there would be no attack. But there were difficult problems to face and much work to do. Smiling, he said: "Forgive me, for coming without getting cleaned up first. Now I have to go right away, there's much to be done."

"Yes," I said. "Don't worry about it; I understand. I'm glad the danger's past and you're all right."

He mentioned that he had been in one of the most dangerous spots. "As always," I responded. I was sure without being told that he had probably been stationed at one of the missile sites.

He always was tenderly concerned for our daughter despite the intense preoccupations. He tried his best to prevent our separation from affecting her. He tried later to visit her once a week, or he sent for her to spend Sundays with him and his new family. When she was older, he used to take her with him to do volunteer work in the fields. In August 1964 the Workers' Confederation of Cuba presented him with a plaque signifying "Vanguard Worker," and when Hildita completed her school year as a "Vanguard Student," her father gave her the plaque.

When he was traveling, he sent her many postcards, or if he found the time, he wrote her short but affectionate letters. On his next to last trip, he went to Africa and for the first time went contrary to custom and sent Hildita a valuable present, a ring with precious stones, with the following note: "In flight, Karachi—Cairo."

My dear:
When you get this note, I'll be in some African country and you'll have passed your ninth birthday. I'm sending you this little present to wear as a reminder of me. I don't know if it's the right size, but it should fit one of your five little fingers.

I miss you so much. I've been away for two months and I know everything is going to be a little bit changed when I see you again.

See if this year you can be a model exemplary student again, and make me proud, and your mama too.

Dear little one, here's a great big kiss and a huge abrazo *from your*
  Papá who loves you.
  Regards to everyone there.

And some of the postcards:

From India

Hildita:
A few lines to send you a big abrazo *from a faraway country that one day you'll know.*

We are working very hard, meeting many people, and doing many interesting things, about which I will tell you when I come back. I have a present for you.
  Your father,
  CHE.

From Yugoslavia

Hildita:
A hug from your father from a grotto here that reminds me of Cacahuamilpa in Mexico, to where you were on your way.
  Affectionate best to your mother.
  ERNESTO.

From Egypt

My girl:
Again I am visiting places that you'll see someday, and thinking of you.
This postcard will probably reach you after I have arrived in Havana, but it will give you an idea of these stone monuments.
Love and kisses from your
Papá

From someplace in Africa

My dear:
Here is a picture of a friend of yours from school. I don't know if you'll recognize him. I am now in Dahomey. Look for it on the map. A hug for everyone and for you a big kiss from your
Papá

Leaving France

Hildita dear:
A kiss for you from high in the air thousands of feet and hundreds of kilometers, high in the air so it will reach you faster.
I love you.
Your old man

From Saudi Arabia

Dear Hilda:
A kiss on the way through Saudi Arabia, land of horses and oil. And another one in advance to the one when I get back. Give my love to your mother.
Papá

From Tanganyika

My dear:
Another memento from your papá, who this time is getting closer to Havana.

> *This is a religious dance of a very proud people who have al-*
> *ways fought for their freedom. A big kiss from your father.*
> *Best to your mother.*

From Bamako, Republic of Mali

> *My dear:*
> *Since I have no news from anyone, and I keep going, I can only send*
> *you a big* abrazo *and tell you that all goes well.*
> *The trip is very interesting because I get to know countries and*
> *people who struggle as we do for a better future.*
> *A kiss from your papá.*
> *Happy New Year.*

THE EVENING BEFORE Ernesto left for New York to head the
Cuban delegation to the United Nations, he came to visit us. We
talked as usual about Latin American subjects, particularly about
the death of Don Pedro Albizu Campos, who had been taken from
prison, unconscious, to die. Ernesto was outraged at this new crime
perpetrated by Yankee imperialism.

I had just received a letter from his father, announcing that he
would soon arrive in Cuba. He hadn't been able to come before because he had suffered an automobile accident. As I told Ernesto
about it, he showed unusual concern, and he asked: "Why didn't he
come . . . ! What a pity! *Now there's no more time.*" He repeated the
last phrase when I insisted his "old man" would make the trip anyway. Only months later did I realize what that sentence meant.

When he returned from the United Nations, he called two or
three times and said that he would come by. He did so once, but I
wasn't there. Several times we waited, but he didn't come, calling
later to apologize and saying that he was very busy.

Then he went to Africa again, from whence came the many
postcards to his daughter. When he returned on March 14,
Hildita went to the airport to greet him, and he brought her

home, continuing on to the city immediately with Fidel, after telling Hildita that he would come by the house later. Two or three days later he called and told me that he would come to talk with me, but at the last moment he called again to say that he had to leave for the countryside to cut sugar cane, and that when he came back from the volunteer work, he would visit me.

ON APRIL 20, 1965, in response to rumors that something had happened to Ernesto, Fidel announced that Che was all right and that he was "where he would be of the most use to the revolution." I was certain that he was in some other country fighting imperialism. That same day Hildita received the first word from him since his "disappearance":

> *Dear daughter:*
> *I am writing you these few words so that you'll know that your old man is always thinking of you.*
>
> *I saw some recent pictures of you and it seems you're becoming a woman; soon we will have to station a guard at the door against suitors.*
>
> *I am a little far away. I'm doing some work that I've been given, and it will be a little while before I can return. Don't forget to go by the house to check on your brothers and sisters, who are a little undisciplined and don't always do their homework.*
>
> *Viejita, until I return or until I find another moment to write you again, I'll be waiting to hear from you. Regards to your mother, to your cousin, and for you, a big hug and kiss. Many thoughts . . . from your*
> *Papá*

Around April 1966 our daughter received from her father this birthday letter:

> *Dear Hildita:*
> *I write knowing that the letter will arrive quite late, but I want you to know that I am thinking of you and hoping that you are happy on*

your birthday. You're almost a woman now, and I can't write to you as to a child, the foolishnesses and little fibs.

I have to tell you that I am still far away, and I'll be away from you for a long time, doing what I can to fight our enemies. It is not much but I'm doing something, and I believe you'll always be able to be proud of your father, as I am of you.

Remember that many years of struggle still lie ahead, and though you're a woman, you'll have to do your part in the fight. Meanwhile, you must prepare, be a true revolutionary, which at your age means to learn a lot, everything you can, and always be ready to support just causes. Also, to obey your mother, and not to try for too much before it's time. The time always comes.

You must strive to be among the best in school, best in all senses. You know what this means: study and maintain the revolutionary attitude, that is, honest behavior, seriousness, love for the revolution, comradeship. I wasn't like that when I was your age, but I was in a different society, where man was the enemy of man. You now enjoy the privilege of living in another time; you must be worthy of it.

Don't forget to go by the house to see the other kids, tell them to study and behave. Give special advice to Aleidita, who minds you very well, you being the older sister.

Well, my little old lady, happy birthday. Give your mother and Gina a hug for me, and a really big one for you, big enough to last till we see each other, from your

Papá

In October 1967, when the news of his death was confirmed, Hildita and her other sisters and brothers received the following message:

TO MY CHILDREN
Dear Hildita, Aleidita, Camilo, Celia and Ernesto:
If you ever have to read this letter, it is because I am with you no longer.

You will hardly remember much about me; the youngest won't remember anything.

Your father has been a man who has acted as he believed, and of a certainty has been true to his convictions.

Grow as good revolutionaries. Study hard so that you can mas-
ter the technique that permits mastery of nature. Remember that the
revolution is the important thing and that each one of us alone is
worth nothing.

Above all, always be capable of feeling most deeply any injustice
committed against anyone, anywhere in the world. This is the most
beautiful quality in a revolutionary.

Until forever, my dear children. I hope I may yet see you. A great
big kiss and a big abrazo *from*
Papá

In the days following the confirmation of his murder, I wrote
a short note about him for the magazine *Casa*, published by Casa
de las Americas. The note was published in the special issue in trib-
ute to his memory in January 1968.

To ERNESTO CHE GUEVARA

With the boom of 21 cannons the farewell was at hand, and I
thought, Ernesto Che Guevara, you are no more, physically you
have ceased to be, exceptional man, revolutionary of integrity,
loving son and father, New Man, who manifested in every act
of your life the revolutionary moral principles that you pro-
claimed, deeply human and brotherly comrade. I recalled the
verses of our great poet César Vallejo, whom you respected and
admired so much, when he spoke of your death and I said with
him:

Ernesto Guevara is dead. They beat him who did nothing
to them
hard with a club and hard
too with a rope; witnesses remain:
Thursdays, arm bones,
loneliness, rain, and the roads . . .
And I could add, they shot him many times when he was
unarmed; they cut off fingers to prove his death. They feared him
even dead because he is a banner of struggle and redemption;
the fields of Bolivia are witnesses, as are the fields of all America, the peasants, the workers, the students, the intellectuals. . . .

You are no longer here in body, Ernesto Che Guevara, but your example is, so is your work, and the principles for which you fell; the unredeemed peoples are still here. Other fighters will take your arms and free our peoples; your blood has fed the hard roads of our revolution in march. You will always be present in our struggles.

And what to say of your heroism? Of that twofold, threefold heroism, on embracing the guerrilla war in an unhospitable jungle—now that the imperialist beast uses every means to deny existence to a new Cuba—with asthma your inseparable companion since you were three years old. If it is heroic for anybody to face these dangers, for somebody like you it is much more. It could only have been done by an iron will and the total conviction that it is "the time of the ovens."

And in spite of our pain and the suffering of all revolutionaries, we who knew you can say that you have faced all the dangers and that you have gone to the fight with joy as always, happy to offer the best of yourself in the struggle for justice. Happy, suffering, and happy, dying, for our ideals, with the happiness of knowing surely that other men win follow your example.

You will always be the guide of the Latin American revolution.

Like Bolívar and Martí you will lead our people to victory.

And although a "shroud of Cuban tears," and tears of the whole continent and the world will be with you in your "passing into American history," there will be with you as well the decision and the unbreakable resolution of all revolutionaries to continue your labors in all fields, in work, in study and in combat.

INDEX